WIREMAN FIRST YEAR MCQ

OBJECTIVE QUESTION ANSWERS

MANOJ DOLE

Digitization is the need of the time. In the future, training in industrial training institutes will need to be conducted using online internet to make training more convenient and easy. E-books containing a set of MCQ questions will be made available to the trainees as they need to be more accustomed to the multiple choice questions MCQ to prepare for the online exams taking place in their industrial training institutes.

With all these factors in mind, Mr. Manoj Madhukar Dole Instructor, Industrial Training Institute, Satara, has written books according to the new annual system and NSQF-5 syllabus. And they've created theoretical mobile apps and blogs to make training easier, and made all these educational materials available for download on the world famous websites Google Play Store, Amazon and Apple Book Store.

The books were published by Hon'ble Joint Director Shri Rajendra Ghume Saheb Regional Office of Vocational Education and Training, Pune on 9/1/2019, at this time Shri Prakash Saigavkar Saheb Principal Government Industrial Training Institute Aundh Pune, Shri Tukaram Misal Saheb Principal Govt. Q. Sanstha Satara, Shri Sachin Dhumal Saheb District Vocational Education and Training Officer Satara, Shri Yatin Pargaonkar Saheb Principal Govt. Q. Sanstha Kolhapur, Shri Vikas Teke Saheb Inspector Vocational Education and Training Regional Office Pune, Palekar Foods Products Pvt. Ltd. Entrepreneurial Chairman of Satara Mr. Nilkanthrao Palekar Saheb, Chairman of Hira Foods Mr. Ibrahim Baba Tamboli Saheb, Mrs. Shalmali Pawar Headmaster Government Technical School Center Satara and other dignitaries were present on the occasion.

Contents

Prologue

Wireman First Year MCQ is a simple Book for ITI Engineering Course Wireman First Year, NSQF-4 Syllabus, It contains objective questions with underlined & bold correct answers MCQ covering all topics including all about safety and environment, use of fire extinguishers, artificial respiratory resuscitation to begin with. He gets the idea of planning & preparing good quality electrical wire joints for single and multi stand conductors suitable for applications with soldering and taking suitable care and safety. The trainee will be able to draw and set up DC and AC circuits including R-L-C circuits with accurate measurement of voltage, current, resistance, power, power factor and energy using ammeter, voltmeter, ohm-meter, watt-meter, energy meter, power factor meter and phase sequence tester with proper care and safety, plan, draw, estimate material, wire up and test different type of domestic wiring circuits as per Indian Electricity rules and taking care of quality, Construction and working of MCB & ELCB. Test a domestic wiring installation using Megger. The trainee will identify the type of batteries, construction, working and application of Ni-cadmium, lithium cell, lead acid cell etc. Demonstrate their charging and discharging, choosing appropriate method and carryout the installation and routine maintenance with due care and safety. He will plan & select to carry out basic jobs of marking out the components for filing, drilling, and riveting, fitting and assembled using different components independently, plan and install Pipe & Plate earthing. Measure earth resistance by earth tester, select and perform electrical/ electronic measurements with appropriate instrument. He should plan and execute electrical illumination system viz. FL tube, HPMV lamp, HPSV lamp, Halogen & metal halide lamp, CFL, LED lamp etc., plan, draw, estimate material, wire up and test different type of industrial wiring circuits as per Indian Electricity rules and taking care of quality. He will be able to plan, draw, estimate material, wire up and test different type of commercial and computer networking wiring circuits as per Indian Electricity rules and taking care of quality, and lots more.

We add new question answers with each new version. Please email us in case of any errors/omissions. This is arguably the largest and best Book for All engineering multiple choice questions and answers.

As a student you can use it for your exam prep. This e-Book is also useful for professors to refresh material.

Foreword

Vocational education and training is imparted through the Department of Vocational Education and Training through the Department of Business Education and Business Practical to supply multi-skilled artisans in line with the rapidly growing demand in the industrial sector in the 21st century. All the occupations within the institutions are important, as the trainees from these occupations develop multi-skills as per the demands of the industry.

with the noble intention of making available MCQ e-books suitable for all businesses, considering that all the examinations in all the industries in the industrial sector are conducted online and include MCQ method questions. Mr. Manoj Madhukar Dole has written a very good e-book on MCQ method as per the new annual syllabus. This e-book will definitely be a guide for all the trainees, trainee candidates, training instructors and others concerned.

The author of the book is Mr. Manoj Madhukar Dole, Instructor Gov. ITI Satara has 17 years of training experience. Written as a new annual pattern, this e-book incorporates modern digital QR Code technology to understand the layout, simple language, and simple syntax, diagrams and videos for each subject. So I am sure that this e-book will definitely be useful for in-depth study and exam practice. The work they have done is certainly commendable.

Mr. Tukaram Misal
Principal Government Industrial Training Institute Satara.

Preface

DGET New Delhi and CSTARI Kolkata have been implementing an annual pattern for all businesses in ITI since the August 2018 session. The examination system will also be changed and it will be online from this year and since all the questions are of Objective Type (MCQ), the trainees are in dire need of in-depth study. It is with this in mind that we are delighted to present the books based on the old NIMI pattern and a complete overview of the new annual pattern, and we hope that these books will be a guide for all business directors and trainees. Is.

For writing these books, Johar Awate Saheb, Principal of ITI Akluj. Former Principal of ITI Satara Saigavkar Saheb, Assistant Director Shri Chandrakant Dhekne Saheb Regional Office of Vocational Education and Training, Pune, District Vocational Education and Training Officer Sachin Dhumal Saheb and Headmaster Government Technical School Kendra Shalmali Pawar Madam and son Adhiraj Dole, mother Kusum Dole, I am very grateful to my father Madhukar Dole and wife Ashwini Dole for their special guidance and cooperation from time to time.

Also, in a very short period of time, the book was reviewed by Shri Rajendra Ghume Saheb, Joint Director, Vocational Education and Training Regional Office, Pune, for his invaluable time in publishing the book. I am sincerely grateful for their feedback.

I am grateful to the Instructor of ITI Satara for there continuous support from the very beginning of writing the book.

From this book, I consider myself blessed to have shared my thoughts on e-learning with you. I will not claim that this book is perfect, because considering the perfection, this book is an attempt and is in its infancy. They will be valuable for improvement if they are tested and suggested.

Manoj Dole
Dated 9/1/2019

Acknowledgements

The industrial training and theoretical examination system of our industrial training institutes and these changes have been accepted by the craft instructors and the trainees. Theoretical examinations conducted in your industrial training institutes are also conducted online. Since these examinations are of multiple choice MCQ method, the trainees will need to get more practice of such questions.

With all these considerations in mind, Mr. Manoj Madhukar, Director, Dole Crafts, Katari Industrial Training Institute, Satara, has done a thorough study and with his diligent work and added his keen intellect, according to the new annual system and NSQF-5 syllabus, e-book of Katari and other machine trades. -Book) and they have created mobile apps and blogs on theoretical topics to make training easier and have made all these educational materials available for download on the world famous websites Google Play Store, Amazon and Apple Book Store. Training has been made easier by creating a print version and using advanced techniques like QR Code.

All these educational materials will definitely be a guide for all the trainees for in-depth study and for the craft instructors and other concerned who are imparting vocational training.

CHAPTER ONE

Wireman First Year QR Code Images

Download App
Online Test Exam
ITI Books
AutoCAD CAM
JOB & Apprentice
Online Theory
Computer Course
Trading Course
CNC Course
MSCIT Course
Shopping Business
Internet Business
Web Designing
Online Services
Top Sportsmans
Indian Army
Freedom Fighters
Top Scientists
Social Reformers
Motivational Speaker
Top Richest People
Join WhatsApp Group
Join Facebook Group
Like Facebook Page
PAN / Adhar / Licence
Passport

2 ITI Book MCQ - Manoj Dole
www.itibook.com
Fire extinguisher
SAFETY FIRST
Calliper
www.itigov.blogspot.com www.jobapprentices.blogspot.com www.ititests.blogspot.com
www.itibook.com

ITI Book MCQ - Manoj Dole
www.itibook.com
Hacksaw frame
Universal surface guage
Hammer
www.itigov.blogspot.com
www.jobapprentices.blogspot.com
www.ititests.blogspot.com
www.itibook.com

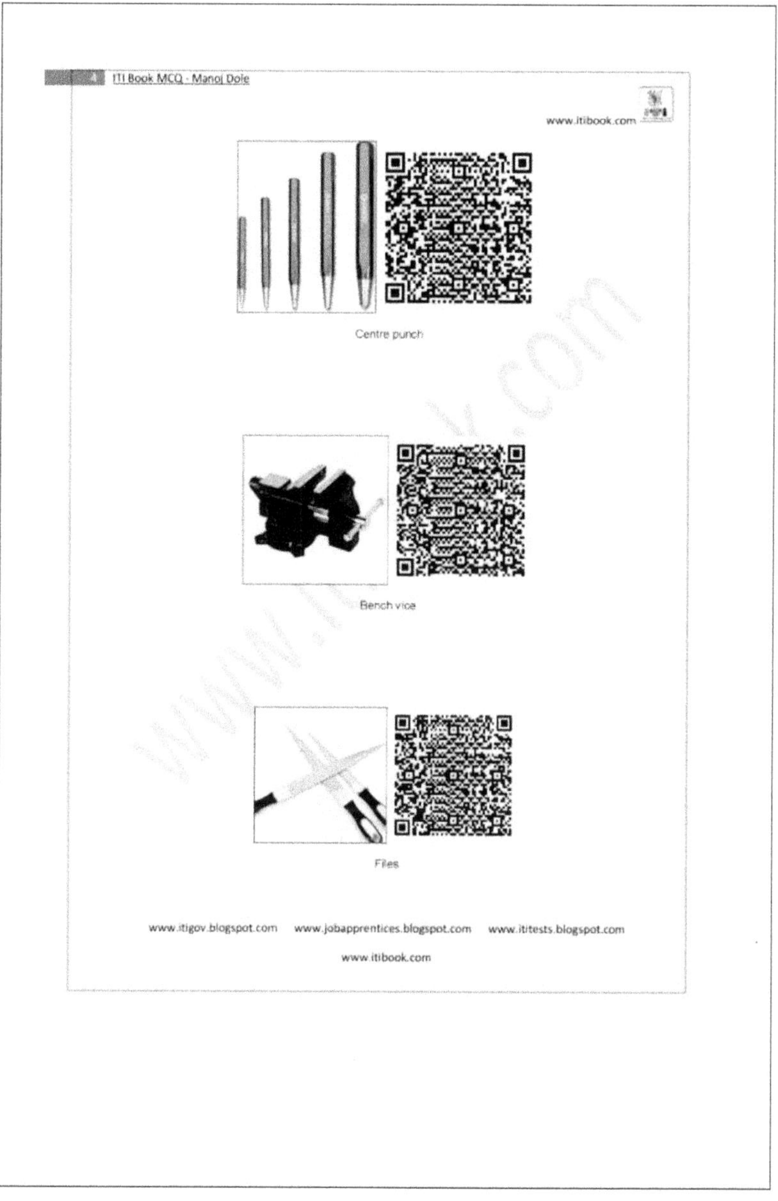
4 ITI Book MCQ - Manoj Dole
www.itibook.com
Centre punch
Bench vice
Files
www.itigov.blogspot.com www.jobapprentices.blogspot.com www.ititests.blogspot.com
www.itibook.com

ITI Book MCQ - Manoj Dole
www.itibook.com
Vernier bevel protractor
www.itigov.blogspot.com www.jobapprentices.blogspot.com www.ititests.blogspot.com
www.itibook.com

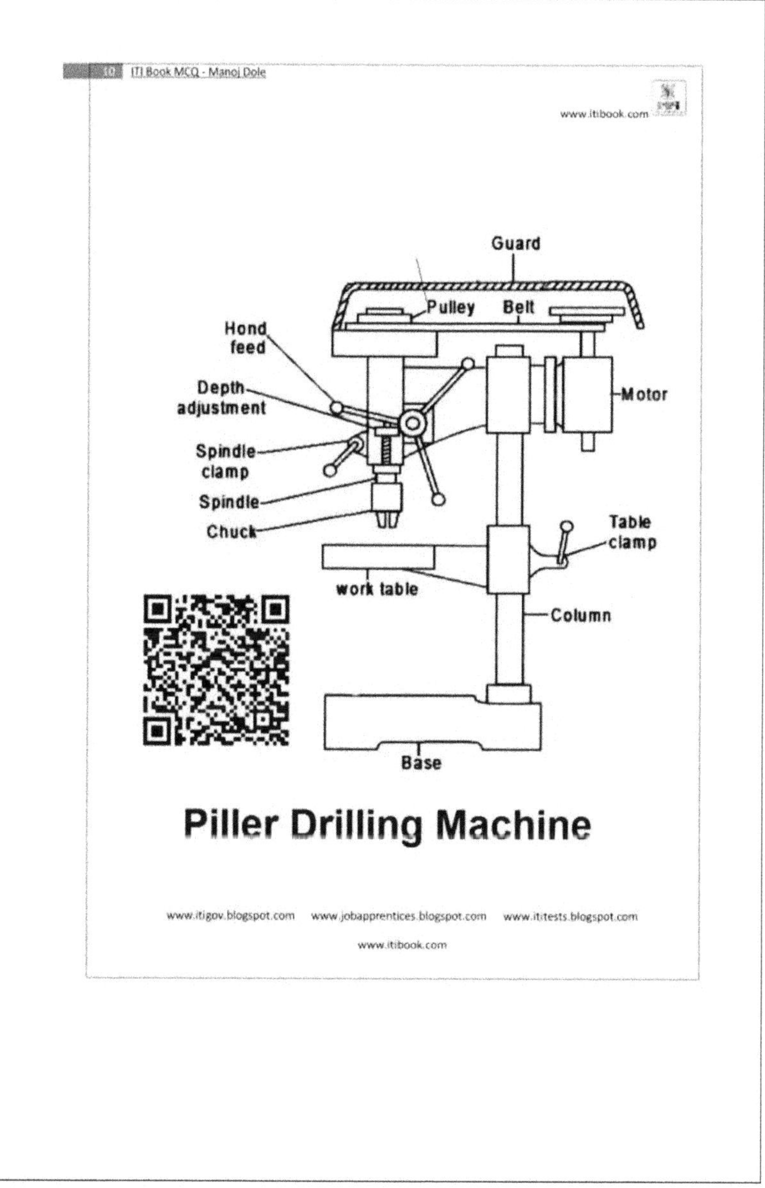
ITI Book MCQ - Manoj Dole
www.itibook.com
Guard
Pulley
Belt
Hond feed
Depth adjustment
Spindle clamp
Spindle
Chuck
Motor
Table clamp
work table
Column
Base
Piller Drilling Machine
www.itigov.blogspot.com
www.jobapprentices.blogspot.com
www.ititests.blogspot.com
www.itibook.com

14 ITI Book MCQ - Manoj Dole
www.itibook.com
battery
capacitor
cell
dynamometer
electromagnet
heater
inductance
magnet
www.itigov.blogspot.com www.jobapprentices.blogspot.com www.ititests.blogspot.com
www.itibook.com

15 ITI Book MCQ - Manoj Dole
www.itibook.com
megger
motor
multimeter
ohmmeter
resistores
star connected
alternator
voltmeter
ammeter
wattmeter
www.itigov.blogspot.com www.jobapprentices.blogspot.com www.ititests.blogspot.com
www.itibook.com

Coffee maker
Blender
Mixer
Toaster
Microwave
Crock pot
Rice cooker
Pressure cooker
Bachelor griller (U.K.)
Stove
Lamp
Light bulb
Lantern
Torch
Clothes iron
Electric drill

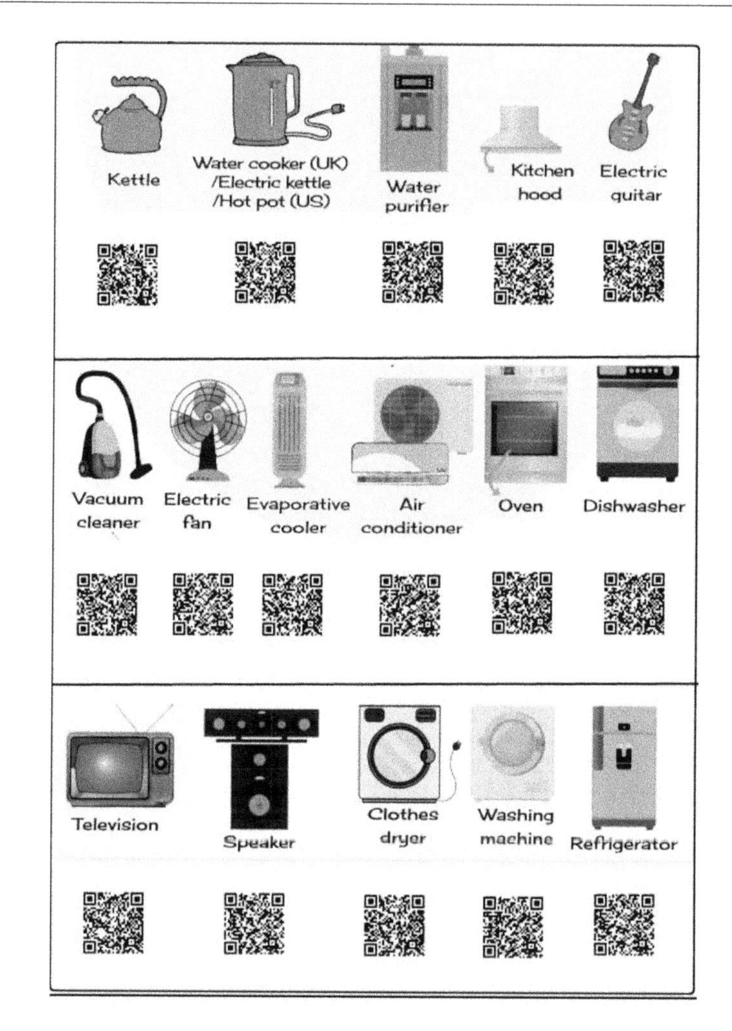
Kettle
Water cooker (UK) /Electric kettle /Hot pot (US)
Water purifier
Kitchen hood
Electric guitar
Vacuum cleaner
Electric fan
Evaporative cooler
Air conditioner
Oven
Dishwasher
Television
Speaker
Clothes dryer
Washing machine
Refrigerator

COMPUTER PARTS
COMPUTER
MOUSE
KEY BOARD
SCREEN / MONITOR
FLASH DRIVE
TOWER
COMPACT DISC
LAPTOP
PRINTER
SCANNER
CARTRIDGES
WEB CAM

COMPUTER PARTS
SPEAKER
HEADPHONES
SMARTPHONE
TABLET / I-PAD
MICROPHONE
WIRELESS ROUTER
MP3 PLAYER
JOYSTICK / GAME

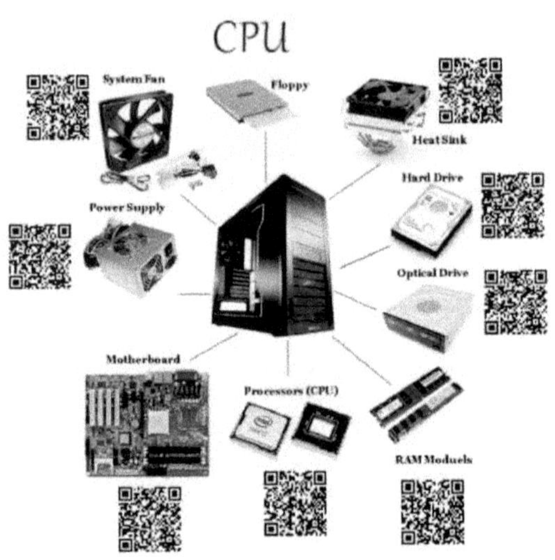

Computer CPU
Hardware Components

Learn DOS Commands
All DOS Command with explanations
MS-DOS
Computer
Operator

topic
Microsoft Access

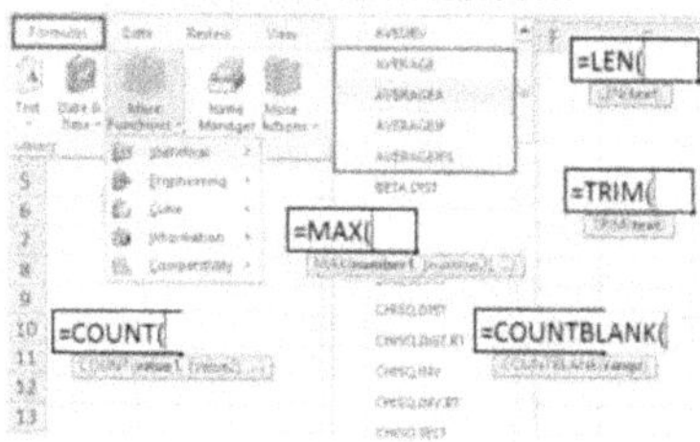
Excel Basic Functions
=LEN(
=TRIM(
=MAX(
=COUNT(
=COUNTBLANK(

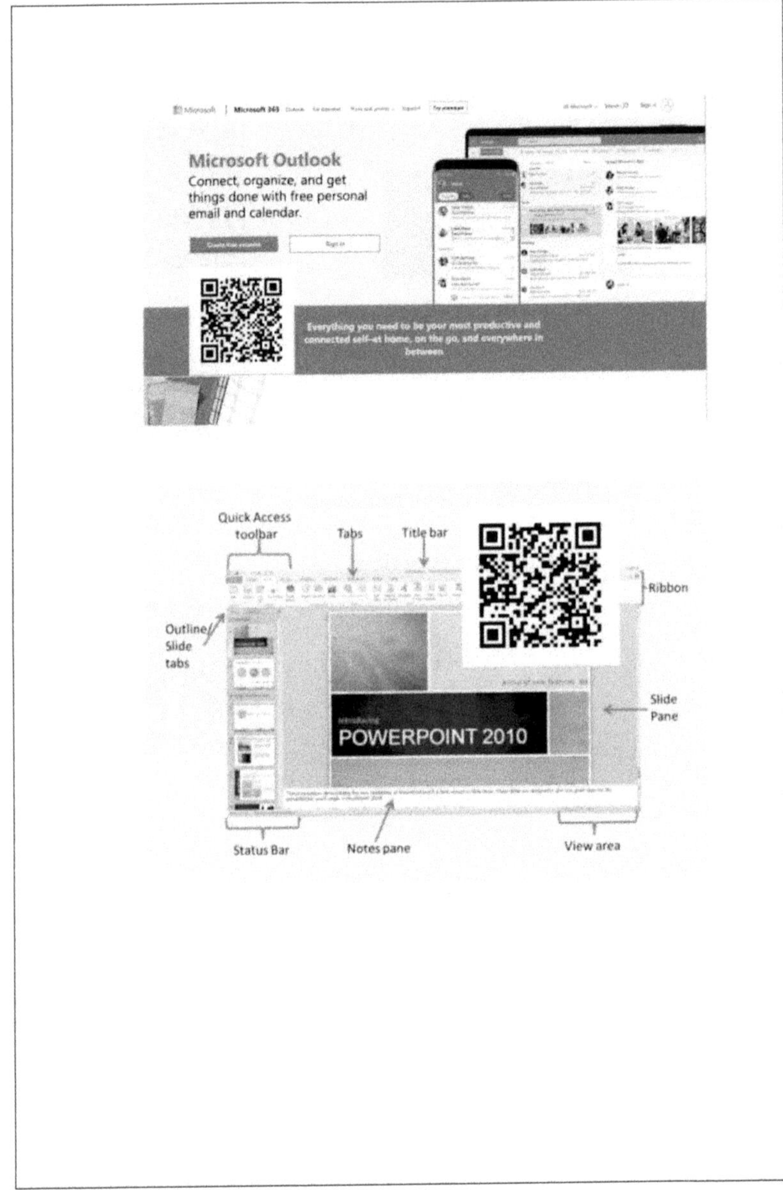
Microsoft Outlook
Connect, organize, and get things done with free personal email and calendar.
Everything you need to be your most productive and connected self–at home, on the go, and everywhere in between
Quick Access toolbar
Tabs
Title bar
Ribbon
Outline/ Slide tabs
Slide Pane
POWERPOINT 2010
Status Bar
Notes pane
View area

MS Paint
Microsoft
FEATURES OF
MS WORD
IN HINDI
W
• WHAT IS MS WORD
• HISTORY OF MS WORD
• FEATURES OF MS WORD
Software Installation

Bluetooth
Bluetooth
Bluetooth
APP
APP
APP
HOST
SDP
RFCOMM
L2CAP
HCI
LM
BR/EDR PHY
CONTROLLER
HOST
SDP
GATT
ATT
SMP
RFCOMM
L2CAP
HCI
LM
LL
BR/EDR + LE PHY
CONTROLLER
GATT
ATT
SMP
L2CAP
HCI
LL
LE PHY
CONTROLLER
Wi Fi
DSL/Cable
Local Network
What is a Browser - Definition and

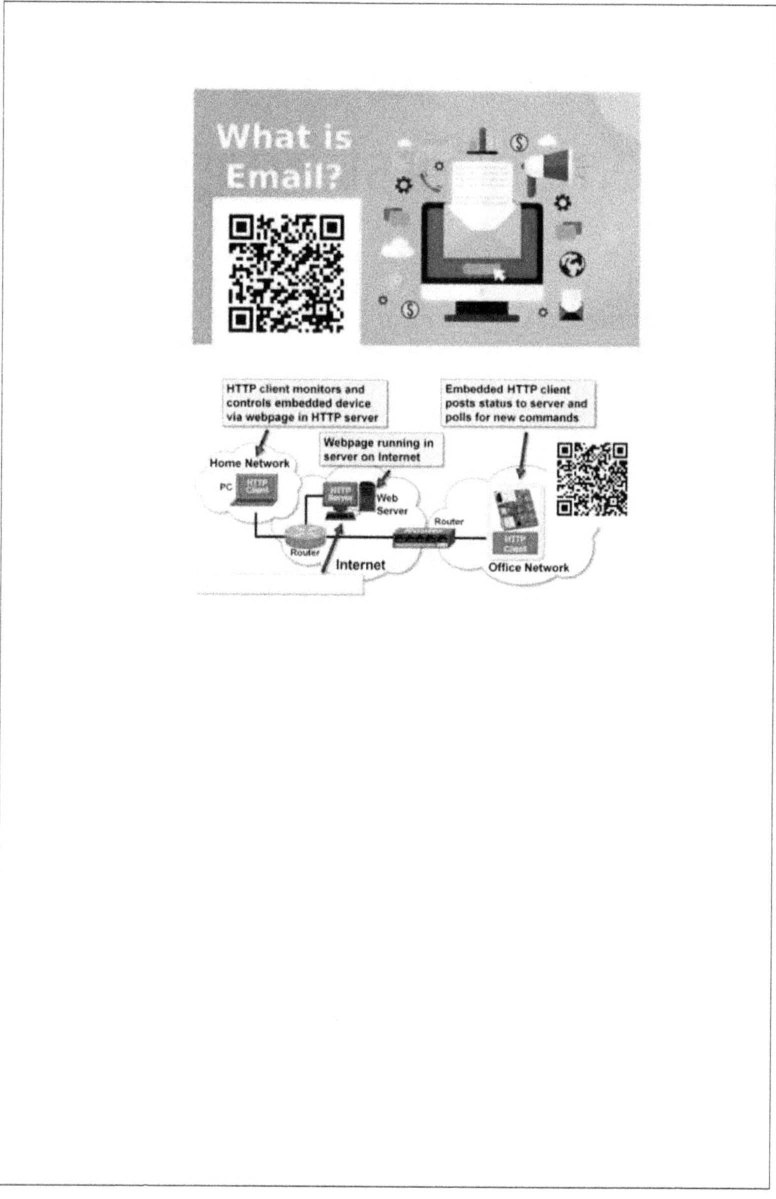
What is
Email?
HTTP client monitors and controls embedded device via webpage in HTTP server
Embedded HTTP client posts status to server and polls for new commands
Webpage running in server on Internet
Home Network
PC
Web Server
Router
Router
Internet
Office Network

CHAPTER TWO

Wireman First Year MCQ

01] In case of bleeding, take treatment Of

D] cold 3" and rest

A] spray cold water

B] Bandage immediately -----

B] Enquire about the accident thought treatment

02] in case of an accident, the victim should im

A] Asked to take rest

C] Attended immediately

D] leave him

03] First aid is given to an injured or ill person primarily

A] Save life

B] Prevent further deterioration of the muff's

C] Give best possible comfort

D] All of these

04] Colour code for Bins for waste paper segregation is -----

A] blue Colour

B] Yellow Colour

C] Red Colour

D] Green Colour

05] In Japanese Seiko stands for -------------

A] Shine

B] Sort

C] Standardize

D] Sustain

06] Benefit of SS system is ------

A] Increase in productivity

B] Increase in quality

C] Reduction in wastage of time

D] All of these

07] Safety is -----------

A] nobody's business

B] every bodise business

C] Some bodies business

D] The organization business

08] For basic categories of safety signs are available The meaning of"prohibition" sign ----

A] shows it must not be done

B] Shows what must be done

C] Warns the hazard or danger

D] Gives information of safety provision

09] Which one is a workshop safety?

A] Keep shop floor clean and free from grease, oil or other slippery materials

B] Stop the machine before changing the speed

C] Don't use cracked or chipped tools

D] Don't try to stop a running machine with hand

10] In Personal Protect Equipment (PPE] HELMET is used to

A] protect head

B] Protect eyes

C] Protect hands

D] Protect ears

11] Which of the following belongs to general safety?

A Have a worker in good attitude

B] The work clean and clear

C] Concentrate on your work

D] Keep the floor and gangways clean and clear

12] While grinding, which is used to protect the eyes?

A] Dark green glass

B] Mask

C] Sun glasses

D] Safety goggles

13] Which of the following is done for machine safety?

A] Check the oil level before starting the machine

B] Do things in a methodical way

C] Keep the floor and gangways clean and clear

D] Don't use dies and scarves

14] ln Personal Protect Equipment (PPE], 'sleeves' is used to protect ----------

A] Face

B] Eyes

C] Ears

D] Hands

15] ABC stands for --------------

A] Automatic Breathing Control

B] Automatic Blood Control

C] Airway Breathing Circulation

D] Automatic Blood Circulation

04] Fire & FIRE EXTINGUISHERS

16] To put off"Class B" fire, the types of fire extinguisher used is

A] dry power

B] Carbon dioxide

C] Jet of water

D] Foam type

17] Which type of fire extinguisher is used to put off general fire?

A] Water type Extinguisher

B] Foam type Extinguisher

C] Dry chemical powder Extinguisher

D] Carbon dioxide (C02] Extinguisher

1. The S.I. unit of power is

(a) Henry

(b) coulomb

(c) watt

(d) watt-hour

2. Electric pressure is also called

(a) resistance

(b) power

(c) voltage

(d) energy

3. The substances which have a large number of free electrons and offer a low

resistance are called

(a) insulators

(b) inductors

(c) semi-conductors

(d) conductors

4. Out of the following which is not a poor conductor ?

(a) Cast iron

(b) Copper

(c) Carbon

(d) Tungsten

5. Out of the following which is an insulating material ?

(a) Copper

(b) Gold

(c) Silver

(d) Paper

6. The property of a conductor due to which it passes current is called

(a) resistance

(b) reluctance

(c) conductance

(d) inductance

7. Conductance is reciprocal of

(a) resistance

(b) inductance

(c) reluctance

(d) capacitance

8. The resistance of a conductor varies inversely as

(a) length

(b) area of cross-section

(c) temperature

(d) resistivity

9. With rise in temperature the resistance of pure metals

(a) increases

(b) decreases

(c) first increases and then decreases

(d) remains constant

10. With rise in temperature the resistance of semi-conductors

(a) decreases

(b) increases

(c) first increases and then decreases

(d) remains constant

11. The resistance of a copper wire 200 m long is 21 Q. If its thickness (diameter)

is 0.44 mm, its specific resistance is around

(a) 1.2 x 10~8 Q-m

(b) 1.4 x 10~8 Q-m

(c) 1.6 x 10″"8 Q-m

(d) 1.8 x 10″8 Q-m

13. An instrument which detects electric current is known as

(a) voltmeter

(b) rheostat

(c) wattmeter

(d) galvanometer

14. In a circuit a 33 Q resistor carries a current of 2 A. The voltage across the resistor is

(a) 33 V

(b) 66 v

(c) 80 V

(d) 132 V

15. A light bulb draws 300 mA when the voltage across it is 240 V. The resistance of the light bulb is

(a) 400 Q

(b) 600 Q

(c) 800 Q

(d) 1000 Q

16. The resistance of a parallel circuit consisting of two branches is 12 ohms. If the resistance of one branch is 18 ohms, what is the resistance of the other ?

(a) 18 Q

(b) 36 Q

(c) 48 Q

(d) 64 Q

17. Four wires of same material, the same cross-sectional area and the same length when connected in parallel give a resistance of 0.25 Q. If the same four wires are connected is series the effective resistance will be

(a) 1 Q

(b) 2 Q

(c) 3 Q

(d) 4 Q

18. A current of 16 amperes divides between two branches in parallel of resistances 8 ohms and 12 ohms respectively. The current in each branch is

(a) 6.4 A, 6.9 A

(b) 6.4 A, 9.6 A

(c) 4.6 A, 6.9 A

(d) 4.6 A, 9.6 A

19. Current velocity through a copper conductor is

(a) the same as propagation velocity of electric energy

(b) independent of current strength

(c) of the order of a few ^.s/m

(d) nearly 3 x 108 m/s

20. Which of the following material has nearly zero temperature co-efficient of resistance?

(a) Manganin

(b) Porcelain

(c) Carbon

(d) Copper

21. You have to replace 1500 Q resistor in radio. You have no 1500 Q resistor but have several 1000 Q ones which you would connect

(a) two in parallel

(b) two in parallel and one in series

(c) three in parallel

(d) three in series

22. Two resistors are said to be connected in series when

(a) same current passes in turn through both

(b) both carry the same value of current

(c) total current equals the sum of branch currents

(d) sum of IR drops equals the applied e.m.f.

23. Which of the following statement is true both for a series and a parallel D.C. circuit?

(a) Elements have individual currents

(b) Currents are additive

(c) Voltages are additive

(d) Power are additive

24. Which of the following materials has a negative temperature co-efficient of resistance?

(a) Copper

(b) Aluminum

(c) Carbon

(d) Brass

25. Ohm's law is not applicable to
(a) vacuum tubes
(b) carbon resistors
(c) high voltage circuits
(d) circuits with low current densities
26. Which is the best conductor of electricity ?
(a) Iron
(b) Silver
(c) Copper
(d) Carbon
27. For which of the following 'ampere second' could be the unit ?
(a) Reluctance
(b) Charge
(c) Power
(d) Energy
28. All of the following are equivalent to watt except
(a) (amperes) ohm
(b) joules/sec.
(c) amperes x volts
(d) amperes/volt
29. A resistance having rating 10 ohms, 10 W is likely to be a
(a) metallic resistor
(b) carbon resistor
(c) wire wound resistor
(d) variable resistor
30. Which one of the following does not have negative temperature co-efficient ?
(a) Aluminium
(b) Paper
(c) Rubber
(d) Mica
31. Varistors are
(a) insulators
(6) non-linear resistors
(c) carbon resistors
(d) resistors with zero temperature coefficient
32. Insulating materials have the function of
(a) preventing a short circuit between conducting wires

(b) preventing an open circuit between the voltage source and the load
(c) conducting very large currents
(d) storing very high currents
33. The rating of a fuse wire is always expressed in
(a) ampere-hours
(b) ampere-volts
(c) kWh
(d) amperes
34. The minimum charge on an ion is
(a) equal to the atomic number of the atom
(b) equal to the charge of an electron
(c) equal to the charge of the number of electrons in an atom (#) zero
35. In a series circuit with unequal resistances
(a) the highest resistance has the most of the current through it
(b) the lowest resistance has the highest voltage drop
(c) the lowest resistance has the highest current
(d) the highest resistance has the highest voltage drop
36. The filament of an electric bulb is made of
(a) carbon
(b) aluminium
(c) tungsten
(d) nickel
37. A 3 Q resistor having 2 A current will dissipate the power of
(a) 2 watts
(b) 4 watts
(c) 6 watts
(d) 8 watts
38. Which of the following statement is true?
(a) A galvanometer with low resistance in parallel is a voltmeter
(b) A galvanometer with high resistance in parallel is a voltmeter
(c) A galvanometer resistance in series is an ammeter with low
(d) A galvanometer with high resistance in series is an ammeter
39. The resistance of a few meters of wire conductor in closed electrical circuit is
(a) practically zero
(b) low
(c) high
(d) very high

40. If a parallel circuit is opened in the main line, the current

(a) increases in the branch of the lowest resistance

(b) increases in each branch

(c) is zero in all branches

(d) is zero in the highest resistive branch

41. If a wire conductor of 0.2 ohm resistance is doubled in length, its resistance becomes

(a) 0.4 ohm

(b) 0.6 ohm

(c) 0.8 ohm

(d) 1.0 ohm

42. Three 60 W bulbs are in parallel across the 60 V power line. If one bulb burns open

(a) there will be heavy current in the main line

(b) rest of the two bulbs will not light

(c) all three bulbs will light

(d) the other two bulbs will light

43. The four bulbs of 40 W each are connected in series swift a battery across them, which of the following statement is true ?

(a) The current through each bulb in same

(b) The voltage across each bulb is not same

(c) The power dissipation in each bulb is not same

(d) None of the above

44. Two resistances Rl and Ri are connected in series across the voltage source where Rl>Ri. The largest drop will be across

(a) Rl

(b) Ri

(c) either Rl or Ri

(d) none of them

46. A closed switch has a resistance of

(a) zero

(b) about 50 ohms

(c) about 500 ohms

(d) infinity

47. The hot resistance of the bulb's filament is higher than its cold resistance because the temperature co-efficient of the filament is

(a) zero

(b) negative

(c) positive

(d) about 2 ohms per degree

49. The insulation on a current carrying conductor is provided

(a) to prevent leakage of current

(b) to prevent shock

(c) both of above factors

(d) none of above factors

50. The thickness of insulation provided on the conductor depends on

(a) the magnitude of voltage on the conductor

(b) the magnitude of current flowing through it

(c) both (a) and (b)

(d) none of the above

51. Which of the following quantities remain the same in all parts of a series circuit ?

(a) Voltage

(b) Current

(c) Power

(d) Resistance

52. A 40 W bulb is connected in series with a room heater. If now 40 W bulb is replaced by 100 W bulb, the heater output will

(a) decrease

(b) increase

(c) remain same

(d) heater will burn out

53. In an electric kettle water boils in 10 m minutes. It is required to boil the boiler in 15 minutes, using same supply mains

(a) length of heating element should be decreased

(b) length of heating element should be increased

(c) length of heating element has no effect on heating if water

(d) none of the above

54. An electric filament bulb can be worked from

(a) D.C. supply only

(b) A.C. supply only

(c) Battery supply only

(d) All above

55. Resistance of a tungsten lamp as applied voltage increases

(a) decreases

(b) increases

(c) remains same
(d) none of the above

56. Electric current passing through the circuit produces
(a) magnetic effect
(b) luminous effect
(c) thermal effect
(d) chemical effect
(e) all above effects

57. Resistance of a material always decreases if
(a) temperature of material is decreased
(6) temperature of material is increased
(c) number of free electrons available become more
(d) none of the above is correct

58. If the efficiency of a machine is to be high, what should be low ?
(a) Input power
(b) Losses
(c) True component of power
(d) kWh consumed
(e) Ratio of output to input

59. When electric current passes through a metallic conductor, its temperature rises. This is due to
(a) collisions between conduction electrons and atoms
(b) the release of conduction electrons from parent atoms
(c) mutual collisions between metal atoms
(d) mutual collisions between conducting electrons

60. Two bulbs of 500 W and 200 W rated at 250 V will have resistance ratio as
(a) 4 : 25
(b) 25 : 4
(c) 2 : 5
(d) 5 : 2

61. A glass rod when rubbed with silk cloth is charged because
(a) it takes in proton
(b) its atoms are removed
(c) it gives away electrons
(d) it gives away positive charge

62. Whether circuit may be AC. or D.C. one, following is most effective in

reducing the magnitude of the current.
(a) Reactor
(b) Capacitor
(c) Inductor
(d) Resistor
63. It becomes more difficult to remove
(a) any electron from the orbit
(6) first electron from the orbit
(c) second electron from the orbit
(d) third electron from the orbit
64. When one leg of parallel circuit is opened out the total current will
(a) reduce
(b) increase
(c) decrease
(d) become zero
65. In a lamp load when more than one lamp are switched on the total resistance
of the load
(a) increases
(b) decreases
(c) remains same
(d) none of the above
66. Two lamps 100 W and 40 W are connected in series across 230 V (alternating).
Which of the following statement is correct ?
(a) 100 W lamp will glow brighter
(b) 40 W lamp will glow brighter
(c) Both lamps will glow equally bright
(d) 40 W lamp will fuse
67. Resistance of 220 V, 100 W lamp will be
(a) 4.84 Q
(b) 48.4 Q
(c) 484 ft
(d) 4840 Q
68. In the case of direct current
(a) magnitude and direction of current remains constant
(b) magnitude and direction of current changes with time
(c) magnitude of current changes with time

(d) magnitude of current remains constant

69. When electric current passes through a bucket full of water, lot of bubbling is

observed. This suggests that the type of supply is

(a) A.C.

(b) D.C.

(c) any of above two

(d) none of the above

70. Resistance of carbon filament lamp as the applied voltage increases.

(a) increases

(b) decreases

(c) remains same

(d) none of the above

71. Bulbs in street lighting are all connected in

(a) parallel

(b) series

(c) series-parallel

(d) end-to-end

72. For testing appliances, the wattage of test lamp should be

(a) very low

(b) low

(c) high

(d) any value

73. Switching of a lamp in house produces noise in the radio. This is because switching operation produces

(a) arcs across separating contacts

(b) mechanical noise of high intensity

(c) both mechanical noise and arc between contacts

(d) none of the above

74. Sparking occurs when a load is switched off because the circuit has high

(a) resistance

(b) inductance

(c) capacitance

(d) impedance

75. Copper wire of certain length and resistance is drawn out to three times its

length without change in volume, the new resistance of wire becomes

(a) 1/9 times

(b) 3 times

(c) 9 times

(d) unchanged

76. When resistance element of a heater fuses and then we reconnect it after removing a portion of it, the power of the heater will

(a) decrease

(b) increase

(c) remain constant

(d) none of the above

77. A field of force can exist only between

(a) two molecules

(b) two ions

(c) two atoms

(d) two metal particles

78. A substance whose molecules consist of dissimilar atoms is called

(a) semi-conductor

(b) super-conducto

(c) compound

(d) insulator

79. International ohm is defined in terms of the resistance of

(a) a column of mercury

(b) a cube of carbon

(c) a cube of copper

(d) the unit length of wire

80. Three identical resistors are first connected in parallel and then in serics.

The resultant resistance of the first combination to the second will be

(a) 9 times

(b) 1/9 times

(c) 1/3 times

(d) 3 times

91. Which method can be used for absolute measurement of resistances ?

(a) Lorentz method

(b) Releigh method

(c) Ohm's law method

(d) Wheatstone bridge method

92. Three 6 ohm resistors are connected to form a triangle. What is the resistance between any two corners ?

(a) 3/2 Q

(b 6 Q

(c) 4 Q

(d) 8/3 Q

93. Ohm's law is not applicable to

(a) semi-conductors

(b) D.C. circuits

(c) small resistors

(d) high currents

94. Two copper conductors have equal length. The cross-sectional area of one conductor is four times that of the other. If the conductor having smaller crosssectional area has a resistance of 40 ohms the resistance of other conductor will be

(a) 160 ohms

(b) 80 ohms

(c) 20 ohms

(d) 10 ohms

95. A nichrome wire used as a heater coil has the resistance of 2 £2/m. For a heater of 1 kW at 200 V, the length of wire required will be

(a) 80 m

(b) 60 m

(c) 40 m

(d) 20 m

96. Temperature co-efficient of resistance is expressed in terms of

(a) ohms/°C

(b) mhos/ohm°C

(c) ohms/ohm°C

98. When current flows through heater coil it glows but supply wiring does not glow because

(a) current through supply line flows at slower speed

(b) supply wiring is covered with insulation layer

(c) resistance of heater coil is more than the supply wires

(d) supply wires are made of superior material

99. The condition for the validity under Ohm's law is that

(a) resistance must be uniform

(b) current should be proportional to the size of the resistance

(c) resistance must be wire wound type

(d) temperature at positive end should be more than the temperature at negative end

100. Which of the following statement is correct ?

(a) A semi-conductor is a material whose conductivity is same as between that of a conductor and an insulator

(b) A semi-conductor is a material which has conductivity having average value of conductivity of metal and insulator

(c) A semi-conductor is one which con¬ducts only half of the applied voltage

(d) A semi-conductor is a material made of alternate layers of conducting material and insulator

101. A rheostat differs from potentiometer in the respect that it

(a) has lower wattage rating

(b) has higher wattage rating

(c) has large number of turns

(d) offers large number of tapping

102. The weight of an aluminium conductor as compared to a copper conductor of identical cross-section, for the same electrical resistance, is

(a) 50%

(b) 60%

(c) 100%

(d) 150%

103. An open resistor, when checked with an ohm-meter reads

(a) zero

(b) infinite

(c) high but within tolerance

(d) low but not zero

104. are the materials having electrical conductivity much less than most of the metals but much greater than that of typical insulators.

(a) Varistors

(b) Thermistor

(c) Semi-conductors

(d) Variable resistors

105. All good conductors have high

(a) conductance

(b) resistance

(c) reluctance

(d) thermal conductivity

106. Voltage dependent resistors are usually made from

(a) charcoal

(b) silicon carbide

(c) nichrome

(d) graphite

107. Voltage dependent resistors are used

(a) for inductive circuits

(b) to supress surges

(c) as heating elements

(d) as current stabilizers

108. The ratio of mass of proton to that of electron is nearly

(a) 1840

(b) 1840

(c) 30

(d) 4

109. The number of electrons in the outer most orbit of carbon atom is

(a) 3

(b) 4

(c) 6

(d) 7

110. With three resistances connected in parallel, if each dissipates 20 W the total power supplied by the voltage source equals

(a) 10 W

(b) 20 W

(c) 40 W

(d) 60 W

111. A thermistor has

(a) positive temperature coefficient

(b) negative temperature coefficient

(c) zero temperature coefficient

(d) variable temperature coefficient

112. If/, R and t are the current, resistance and time respectively, then according

to Joule's law heat produced will be proportional to

(a) I2Rt

(b) I2Rf

(c) I2R2t

(d) I2R2t*

113. Nichrome wire is an alloy of

(a) lead and zinc

(b) chromium and vanadium

(c) nickel and chromium

(d) copper and silver

114. When a voltage of one volt is applied, a circuit allows one micro ampere current to flow through it. The conductance of the circuit is

(a) 1 n-mho

(b) 106 mho

(c) 1 milli-mho

(d) none of the above

115. Which of the following can have negative temperature coefficient ?

(a) Compounds of silver

(6) Liquid metals

(c) Metallic alloys

(d) Electrolytes

116. Conductance : mho ::

(a) resistance : ohm

(b) capacitance : henry

(c) inductance : farad

(d) lumen : steradian

117. 1 angstrom is equal to

(a) 10-8 mm

(b) 10″6 cm

(c) 10″10 m

(d) 10~14 m

118. One newton meter is same as

(a) one watt

(b) one joule

(c) five joules

(d) one joule second

85] A heater draws a current of 8A when connected to a 240V source] What is the resistance value of the heater element in ohms?

A] 40

B] 20

C] 30

D] 60

86] An electric soldering iron with an 80 ohms heating element is plugged into a 240V outlet] How much current will be drawn by the iron?

A] 2A

B] 3A

C] 4A

D] 5A

87] The alternator in a car delivers 4A and has a load of 3 ohms connected across its terminals] Find the voltage of the circuit

A] 18V

B] 24V

C] 12V

D] 16V

88] Three resistors of 1K ohms, 2K ohms and 7K ohms are connected in series with a 30 V supply] If 2 K ohms and 7 K ohms resistors are open circuited, a voltmeter connected across the 7K ohms resistor will indicate...

A] 10 k ohms, 3A

B] 10 k ohms, 300mA

C] 10 k ohms, 3 mA

D] 5 k ohms, 6 mA

89] A voltage source produces an IR drop of 40V across a 20 ohms resistance, 60V across a 30 ohms resistance and 180V across a 90 ohms resistance all in series] How much is the applied voltage?

A] 180 V

B] 240 V

C] 100 V

D] 280 V

90] Three resistors 27 ohms, 47 ohms and 68 ohms are connected in parallel] What is the otal resistance?

A] less than 27 ohms

B] greater than 68 ohms

C] between 27 and 47 ohms

D] sum of all the three resistances

91] One million and one mege ohms resistors are there if connected both in parallel, what would be the combined resistance value?

A] 0.5 mega ohm

B] 0.5 milli ohm

C] 0.5 kilo ohm

D] 0.5 ohm

92] A 24 ohms and a 8 ohms resistors in parallel gets a combined resistance of...

A] 6 ohms

B] 12 ohms

C] 3 ohms

D] 32 ohms

93] Resistors of the following values are connected in parallel, 5 ohms, 5 kilo-ohms, 50 kilo-ohms, 5 mega ohms] Their equivalent resistance will be very near to...

A] 4.5 ohms

B] 4500 ohms

C] 45000 ohms

D] 4,500,000 ohms

94] The resistance of given wire is 2 ohms] The resistance of the other wire made of the same material having twice the length and twice the cross sectional area is...

A] 5 ohms

B] 6 ohms

C] 2 ohms

D] 8 ohms

95] If the area of a metal wire of a given length is doubles, its resistance will...

A] be doubled

B] be halved

C] remain the same

D] be four times more

96].Among the following only one is regarded as resistance wire

A] gold

B] silver

C] nichrome

D] copper

97] Arc heating occurs when the air between electrodes of opposite polarity becomes..

A] moistened

B] dry

C] ionized

D] none of the above

98] The meter used to measure the temperature of furnace is...

A] hydrometer
B] pyrometer
C] hygrometer
D] tachometer
99] in the case of electrolyte a rise in temperature causes...
A] decrease in resistance
B] increase in resistance
C] no change in resistance
D] none of the above
100] Heat developed in a conductor is proportional to the...
A] square of the power
B] square of the resistance
C] square of the current
D] square of the time
101] Out of the four metal/alloys given below, one has almost no change in resistance for temperature change...
A] nickel
B] nichrome
C] platinum
D] manganin
102] A material that is slightly repelled by a magnet is called ...
A] magnetic
B] paramagnetic
C] diamagnetic
D] ferromagnetic
103] A material that can be magnetized only very slightly is called...
A] magnetic
B] paramagnetic
C] diamagnetic
D] ferromagnetic
104] Substances that can be magnetized easily and make very strong magnets are called...
A] ferromagnetic
B] diamagnetic
C] paramagnetic
D] permanent magnetic
105] A substance that has a high retentivity can be used for the manufacture of...

A] electromagnets

B] permanent magnets

C] temporary magnets

D] paramagnets

106] A substance that has low retentivity can be used for the manufacture of...

A] electromagnets

B] permanent magnets

C] bar magnets

D] paramagnets

107] The symbol for inductance is...

A] H

B] I

C] L

D] X

108] Tube lamp choke is the best example of...

A] open circuited

B] short circuited

C] grounded

D] connected to the neutral line

109] The initial function of a choke in a tube light circuit is to...

A] limit the starting current

B] induce high voltage

C] heat up the filament

D] limit the current after starting

110] The second function of a choke in a tube light circuit is to...

A] limit the starting current

B] induce high voltage

C] heat up the filament

D] limit the current after starting

111] The periodic time of a wave from is 2ms] Calculate the frequency

A] 50 HZ

B] 5 HZ

C] 500HZ

D] 5 KHZ

112] How big is the peak amplitude of a sine-wave with an effective value of 220 volts?

A] 311 V

B] 380 V

C] 400 V

D] 440 V

113] The peak-to-peak voltage is 99V] how big is the effective value of the sine wave?

A] 70 V

B] 44.5V

C] 49.5 V

D] 35 V

114] A moving coil voltmeter reads 10 V AC] How big is the effective voltage?

A] higher

B] lower

C] the same

D] 10% higher

115] A moving iron ammeter reads 10 A] how big is the peak current of the oscillation?

A] 7.07 A

B] 1.1414A

C] 70.7 A

D] 14.1 A

116] A current of 2 amps flows through a resistance of 10 ohms] The power dissipated in the resistance is equal to...

A] 20 watts

B] 200 watts

C] 40 watts

D] 5 watts

117] If the frequency changes from 50 HZ to 100 HZ keeping voltage constant, the inductive reactance of coil connected to supply...

A] remains same

B] become half

C] become doubled

D] become 4 times

118] Capacitance is not affected by...

A] plate area

B] distance between plates

C] dialectic material

D] frequency

119] The capacitive reactance of a capacitor varies...

A] directly with frequency

B] inversely with frequency

C] directly with applied voltage

D] inversely with applied voltage

120] A capacitor acquired 3 coulombs of charge when 6 volts are applied across it] It has a capacitance of ...

A] 0.5 farad

B] 3 farads

C] 3 farads

D] 18 farads

121] A capacitor is connected across a 200 volt AC line, its minimum voltage rating should be...

A] 100 volts

B] 200 Volts

C] 300 volts

D] 400 volts

122] when testing a capacitor with an ohmmeter, the meter indicates some resistance] The capacitor under test is...

A] leaky

B] open

C] good

D] short

123] The total capacitance of a 40 micro farad capacitor connected in series with an 80 micro farad capacitor is...

A] 26.7 micro farad

B] 40 micro farad

C] 60.6 micro farad

D] 120 micro farad

124] For obtaining 1 micro farad capacitor from 3 nos] of 3 micro farad capacitors we have to connect...

A] all in parallel

B] all in series

C] 2 series and one in parallel

D] none of the above

125] In an AC series circuit having R and C the current flowing through the capacitor will be...

A] lagging the voltage

B] leading the voltage

C] in phase with the voltage

D] none of the above

126] If the frequency of the supply is increased in the R-C series circuit the capacitive reactance will be

A] reduced

B] increased

C] having no effect

D] none of the above

127] Power companies are interested in improving the power factor to

A] reduce line current

B] increase motor efficiency

C] increase volt-amperes

D] decrease power

128] A capacitor increases the power factor value of an AC motor load when it is connected...

A] in series with the motor

B] in series with the starter

C] in parallel with the motor

D] in series with the main winding

129] Normally, the power factor of an incandescent lighting circuit is..

A] 0

B] 0.5

C] 0.707

D] 1.0

130] When resistance alone is used to determine current in an RLC series circuit, the circuit is...

A] an inductive circuit

B] a capacitive circuit

C] a combination circuit

D] a resonant circuit

131] Inductive reactance is directly related to..

A] resistance

B] frequency

C] capacitance

D] power

132] Synchronous motor when used for power factor improvement should be...

A] under excited
B] over excited
C] loaded
D] running at no load
133] In a RL parallel circuit, the opposition to total current is called...
A] reactance
B] resistance
C] a vector sum
D] impedance
134] In a AC parallel RL circuit, the power dissipated at the
A] impedance
B] resistance
C] inductance
D] capacitance
135] How much is the nominal output voltage of a carbon zinc cell?
A] 12V
B] 1.5V
C] 2.0V
D] 2.2V
136] Cells are connected in series to..
A] increase the output voltage
B] decreases the output voltage
C] decrease the internal resistance
D] increase the current capacity
54137connected in
A] series
B] parallel
C] series-parallel
D] parallel-series
138] The capacity of a cell is measured in
A] watt-hour
B] watts
C] amperes
D] ampere-hour
139] The primary cell which has the shortest shelf life is
A] carbon – zinc
B] alkaline
C] mercury

D] lithium

140] The cell which has very high energy density for given weight or volume to

A] carbon-zinc

B] alkaline

C] mercury

D] lithium

141] A 100-Ah capacity battery should deliver a current of 8A for approximately...

A] 12 h

B] 8 h

C] 20 h

D] 100 h

142] When the battery is needed to be kept idle for a long time...

A] overcharge the battery

B] remove electrolyte

C] clean the plates with distilled water

D] dry them and store the battery in cool dry clean place

143] The active materials of the nickel iron cell are...

A] nickel hydroxide

B] powdered iron and its oxide

C] 21% solution of caustic potash

D] all the above materials

144] The capacity of a cell is measured in

A] watt hour

B] watts

C] amperes

D] ampere-hour

145] To charge a secondary cell, the system used is

A] low voltage AC

B] high voltage AC

C] AC

D] DC

146] What is the number of phases in a normal industrial supply system?

A] one

B] three

C] four

D] two

147] In a 3 phase star connected alternator, the coils have a phase difference of...

A] 120◦

B] 240◦

C] 60◦

D] 360◦

148] Delta connection is used no one of the following

A] primary of the transmission line transformer

B] alternator winding

C] secondary of the distribution transformer

D] primary of the distribution transformer

149] Which method can be used to measure the power in a 3-phase unbalanced load system?

A] one wattmeter method

B] tow wattmeter method

C] three wattmeter method

D] three ammeter method

150] Two wattmeters can be used to measure 3-hase power in a 3-phase, 3 wire system with...

A] balanced load

B] unbalanced load

C] balanced as well as unbalanced load

D] out of balanced load

151] A single wattmeter can be used to measure power in a 3-phase system only when the load is..

A] balanaced

B] unbalanced

C] balanced as well as unbalanced load

D] constant

152] The force producing movement of the pointer in an indicating instrument is called as...

A] deflecting force

B] controlling force

C] damping force

D] distracting force

153] A permanent magnet moving coil instrument will read...

A] only AC quantities

B] only DC quantities

C] both AC and DC quantities

D] pulsating quantities

154] An instrument using gravity control will read correctly if used in..

A] vertical position only

B] horizontal position only

C] inclined position only

D] any position

155] Which one of the following damping methods is used in permanent magnet moving coil instrument?

A] air damping

B] fluid damping

C] spring damping

D] eddy current damping

156] Moving coil instrument works on the effect of...

A] chemical effect

B] heating effect

C] electrostatic effect

D] electromagnetic effect

157] The meter installed at your house to measure electrical energy is an example of...

A] indication type instrument

B] recording type instrument

C] indicating as well as recording type instrument

D] integrating type instrument

158].Which of the following material is preferred for permanent magnet?

A] alnico

B] y-alloy

C] silicon steel

D] wrought iron

159] The instrument which could be classified as absolute instrument is...

A] milli ammeter

B] micro ammeter

C] galvanometer

D] tangent galvanomer

160] Which of the following methods of damping is commonly used in moving iron instrument?

A] Air damping

B] fluid damping

C] eddy current damping

D] viscosity damping

161] The deflecting torque of a moving iron instrument is directly proportional to the..

A] current

B] square of the current

C] square root of the current

D] voltage

162]Which of the following is used for measuring the medium resistance directly?

A] ammeter

B] megger

C] ohmmeter

D] voltmeter

163] An ohmmeter is used for measuring the...

A] insulation resistance

B] resistance

C] current

D] potential difference

164] Which of the following components is not a part of an ohmmeter?

A] fixed resistor

B] variable resistor

C] capacitor

D] battery

165] In shunt ohmmeter, maximum deflection signifies ..

A] maximum resistance

B] minimum resistance

C] a fault in the megger

D] none of these

166].An unknown DC voltage is to be measured, which measuring range will you select first?

A] 500V

B] 50V

C] 1.5 V

D] 0.5V

167].An unknown direct current of micro ampere rating is to be measured, which measuring range will you select first?

A] 20 micro amp

B] 15 micro amp

C] 150 micro amp

D] 500 micro amp

168] A multimeter cannot measure...

A] current

B] potential difference

C] capacitance

D] resistance

169] Dynamometer type meters are used to measure...

A] only AC quantities

B] only DC quantities

C] both AC and DC

D] pulsating AC only

170] Which effect is used in wattmeter?

A] electrodynamic effect

B] thermal effect

C] chemical effect

D] electrostatic effect

171] Which of the instrument listed below operates efficiently as wattmeter in both AC and DC?

A] PMMC instrument

B] dynamometer instrument

C] hot wire instrument

D] MI instrument

172] Electrodynamic type of instrument are used commonly for the measurement of...

A] voltage

B] current

C] resistance D]

173] When the phase and neutral of the energy meter are interchanged, its disc...

A] rotates in reverse direction

B] rotates in correct direction

C] will stop

D] rotates slowly

E] rotates at high speed

174] When the disc of energy meter is rotating even without connecting any load, the error is called

A] creeping error

B] phase error

C] friction error

D] temperature error

175] AC single phase energy meters record the energy in the unit of...

A] kilowatt hours

B] number of thousands of disc rotation

C] volt amperes

D] kilo volt ampere

176] A megger measures resistance in...

A] ohms

B] hundreds of ohms

C] thousands of ohms

D] millions of ohms

177] A megger is exclusively designed for measuring..

A] very high resistance

B] very low resistance

C] ground faults in power lines

D] over loads on DC motors

178] For pipe earthing the minimum internal diameter of galvanized iron of steel pipe required is...

A] 12.5 mm

B] 16mm

C] 3.5 mm

D] 4 m

179] The earth conductor provides a path to ground for..

A] leakage current

B] over current

C] high voltage

D] circuit current

180] if the size of the circuit copper conductor is 10 sq-mm then the size of earth conductor in G.I] wire should be...

A] 1.5 sq.mm

B] 2.5 sq.mm

C] 5 sq.mm

D] 10 sq.mm

181] One calory is equal to,,,

A] 4187 joules

B] 418.7 joules

C] 41.87 joules

D] 4.187 joules

182] The operating temperature range of electrical stove with bare heating element is...

A] 300◦ to 400◦C

B] 500◦ to 600◦C

C] 550◦ to 900◦C

D] 1100◦ to 1300◦C

183] Which appliance works on heating effect of electric current?

A] incandescent lamp

B] bimetallic thermostat

C] H R C fuse

D] toaster

184] What is the size of nichrome wire for heating element of 1000 watts, 230V heater at 500◦C?

A] 18 SWG

B] 20SWG

C] 24 SWG

D] 25 SWG

185] The heat proof insulating material used for heater base is...

A] mica

B] porcelain

C] asbestos

D] glass wool

186].The temperature regulating component of an automatic electric iron is...

A] heating element

B] thermostat

C] sole plate

D] pressure plate

187].The bread toasting zone temperature is about...

A] 400◦C

B] 800◦C

C] 260◦C

D] 975◦C

188] If a winding makes electrical contact with the metal case of the mixer motor the winding is...

A] grounded

B] open circuited

C] short circuited

D] loose connected

189] If the end shafts of a rotor turns blue it is an indication of...

A] scoring

B] overheating

C] freezing

D] burring

190] What type of motor is used in a food mixer?

A] DC shunt motor

B] universal motor

C] capacitor start motor

D] capacitor start and run motor

191] In what position is the motor mounted in most of the mixers?

A] vertical

B] horizontal

C] inclined

D] parallel

1. The insulating material for a cable should have

(a) low cost

(b) high dielectric strength

(c) high mechanical strength

(d) all of the above

2. Which of the following protects a cable against mechanical injury ?

(a) Bedding

(b) Sheath

(c) Armouring

(d) None of the above

3. Which of the following insulation is used in cables ?

(a) Varnished cambric

(b) Rubber

(c) Paper

(d) Any of the above

4. Empire tape is
(a) varnished cambric
(b) vulcanised rubber
(c) impregnated paper
(d) none of the above

5. The thickness of the layer of insulation on the conductor, in cables, depends upon
(a) reactive power
(b) power factor
(c) voltage
(d) current carrying capacity

6. The bedding on a cable consists of
(a) hessian cloth
(b) jute
(c) any of the above
(d) none of the above

7. The insulating material for cables should
(a) be acid proof
(b) be non-inflammable
(c) be non-hygroscopic
(d) have all above properties

8. In a cable immediately above metallic sheath ______ is provided.
(a) earthing connection
(b) bedding
(c) armouring
(d) none of the above

9. The current carrying capacity of cables in D.C. is more thanthat in A.C. mainly due to
(a) absence of harmonics
(b) non-existence of any stability limit
(c) smaller dielectric loss
(d) absence of ripples
(e) none of the above

10. In case of three core flexible cable the colour of the neutral is
(a) blue
(b) black
(c) brown
(d) none of the above

11 cables are used for 132 kV lines.
(a) High tension
(b) Super tension
(c) Extra high tension
(d) Extra super voltage
12. Conduit pipes are normally used to protect ______ cables.
(a) unsheathed cables
(b) armoured
(c) PVC sheathed cables
(d) all of the above
13. The minimum dielectric stress in a cable is at
(a) armour
(b) bedding
(c) conductor surface
(d) lead sheath
14. In single core cables armouring is not done to
(a) avoid excessive sheath losses
(b) make it flexible
(c) either of the above
(d) none of the above
15. Dielectric strength of rubber is around
(a) 5 kV/mm
(b) 15 kV/mm
(c) 30 kV/mm
(d) 200 kV/mm
16. Low tension cables are generally used up to
(a) 200 V
(b) 500 V
(c) 700 V
(d) 1000 V
17. In a cable, the maximum stress under operating conditions is at
(a) insulation layer
(b) sheath
(c) armour
(d) conductor surface
18. High tension cables are generally used up to
(a) 11kV
(b) 33kV

(c) 66 kV
(d) 132 kV
19. The surge resistance of cable is
(a) 5 ohms
(b) 20 ohms
(c) 50 ohms
(d) 100 ohms
20. PVC stands for
(a) polyvinyl chloride
(b) post varnish conductor
(c) pressed and varnished cloth
(d) positive voltage conductor
21. In the cables, the location of fault is usually found out by comparing
(a) the resistance of the conductor
(b) the inductance of conductors
(c) the capacitances of insulated conductors
(d) all above parameters
22. In capacitance grading of cables we use a _______ dielectric.
(a) composite
(b) porous
(c) homogeneous
(d) hygroscopic
23. Pressure cables are generally not used beyond
(a) 11 kV
(b) 33 kV
(c) 66 kV
(d) 132 kV
24. The material for armouring on cable is usually
(a) steel tape
(b) galvanised steel wire
(c) any of the above
(d) none of the above
25. Cables, generally used beyond 66 kV are
(a) oil filled
(b) S.L. type
(c) belted
(d) armoured
26. The relative permittivity of rubber is

(a) between 2 and 3
(b) between 5 and 6
(c) between 8 and 10
(d) between 12 and 14

27. Solid type cables are considered unreliable beyond 66 kV because
(a) insulation may melt due to higher temperature
(b) skin effect dominates on the conductor
(c) of corona loss between conductor and sheath material
(d) there is a danger of breakdown of insulation due to the presence of voids

28. If the length of a cable is doubled, its capacitance
(a) becomes one-fourth
(b) becomes one-half
(c) becomes double
(d) remains unchanged

29. In cables the charging current
(a) lags the voltage by 90°
(b) leads the voltage by 90°
(c) lags the voltage by 180°
(d) leads the voltage by 180°

30. A certain cable has an insulation of relative permittivity 4. If the insulation is
replaced by one of relative permittivity 2, the capacitance of the cable will become
(a) one half
(6) double
(c) four times
(d) none of the above

31. If a cable of homogeneous insulation has a maximum stress of 10 kV/mm,
then the dielectric strength of insulation should be
(a) 5 kV/mm
(b) 10 kV/mm
(c) 15 kV/mm
(d) 30 kV/mm

32. In the cables, sheaths are used to
(a) prevent the moisture from entering the cable
(b) provide enough strength

(e) provide proper insulation
(d) none of the above
33. The intersheaths in the cables are used to
(a) minimize the stress
(b) avoid the requirement of good insulation
(c) provide proper stress distribution
(d) none of the above
34. The electrostatic stress in underground cables is
(a) same at the conductor and the sheath
(b) minimum at the conductor and maximum at the sheath
(c) maximum at the conductor and minimum at the sheath
(d) zero at the conductor as well as on the sheath
(e) none of the above
35. The breakdown of insulation of the cable can be avoided economically by the
use of
(a) inter-sheaths
(b) insulating materials with different dielectric constants
(c) both (a) and (b)
(d) none of the above
36. The insulation of the cable decreases with
(a) the increase in length of the insulation
(b) the decrease in the length of the insulation
(c) either (a) or (b)
(d) none of the above
37. A cable carrying alternating current has
(a) hysteresis losses only
(b) hysteresis and leakage losses only
(c) hysteresis, leakage and copper losses only
(d) hysteresis, leakage, copper and friction losses
38. In a cable the voltage stress is maximum at
(a) sheath
(6) insulator
(e) surface of the conductor
(d) core of the conductor
39. Capacitance grading of cable implies
(a) use of dielectrics of different permeabilities
(b) grading according to capacitance of cables per km length

(c) cables using single dielectric in different concentrations

(d) capacitance required to be introduced at different lengths to counter the effect

of inductance

40. Underground cables are laid at sufficient depth

(a) to minimise temperature stresses

(b) to avoid being unearthed easily due to removal of soil

(c) to minimise the effect of shocks and vibrations due to gassing vehicles, etc.

(d) for all of the above reasons

41. The advantage of cables over overhead transmission lines is

(a) easy maintenance

(b) low cost

(c) can be used in congested areas

(d) can be used in high voltage circuits

42. The thickness of metallic shielding on cables is usually

(a) 0.04 mm

(b) 0.2 to 0.4 mm

(e) 3 to 5 mm

(d) 40 to 60 mm

43. Cables for 220 kV lines are invariably

(a) mica insulated

(b) paper insulated

(c) compressed oil or compressed gas insulated

(d) rubber insulated

(e) none of the above

44. Is a cable is to be designed for use on 1000 kV, which insulation would you prefer ?

(a) Polyvinyle chloride

(b) Vulcanised rubber

(c) Impregnated paper

(d) Compressed SFe gas

45. If a power cable and a communication cable are to run parallel the minimum

distance between the two, to avoid interference, should be

(a) 2 cm

(b) 10 cm

(c) 50 cm

(d) 400 cm

46. Copper as conductor for cables is used as

(a) annealed

(b) hardened and tempered

(c) hard drawn

(d) alloy with chromium

47. The insulating material should have

(a) low permittivity

(b) high resistivity

(c) high dielectric strength

(d) all of the above

48. The advantage of oil filled cables is

(a) more perfect impregnation

(b) smaller overall size

(c) no ionisation, oxidation and formation of voids

(d) all of the above

49. The disadvantage with paper as insulating material is

(a) it is hygroscopic

(6) it has high capacitance

(c) it is an organic material

(d) none of the above

50. The breakdown voltage of a cable depends on

(a) presence of moisture

(b) working temperature

(c) time of application of the voltage

(d) all of the above

1. "The mass of an ion liberated at an electrode is directly proportional to the quantity of electricity".

The above statement is associated with

(a) Newton's law

(b) Faraday's law of electromagnetic

(c) Faraday's law of electrolysis

(d) Gauss's law

2. The charge required to liberate one gram equivalent of any substance is known as _______ constant

(a) time

(b) Faraday's

(c) Boltzman

3. During the charging of a lead-acid cell

(a) its voltage increases

(b) it gives out energy

(c) its cathode becomes dark chocolate brown in colour

(d) specific gravity of H2SO4 decreases

4. The capacity of a lead-acid cell does not depend on its

(a) temperature

(b) rate of charge

(c) rate of discharge

(d) quantity of active material

5. During charging the specific gravity of the electrolyte of a lead-acid battery

(a) increases

(b) decreases

(c) remains the same

(d) becomes zero

6. The active materials on the positive and negative plates of a fully charged leadacid battery are

(a) lead and lead peroxide

(b) lead sulphate and lead

(c) lead peroxide and lead

(d) none of the above

7. When a lead-acid battery is in fully charged condition, the colour of its positive

plate is

(a) dark grey

(b) brown

(c) dark brown

(d) none of above

8. The active materials of a nickel-iron battery are

(a) nickel hydroxide

(6) powdered iron and its oxide

(c) 21% solution of KOH

(d) all of the above

9. The ratio of ampere-hour efficiency to watt-hour efficiency of a lead-acid cell is

(a) just one

(b) always greater than one

(c) always less than one

(d) none of the above.

10. The best indication about the state of charge on a lead-acid battery is given by

(a) output voltage

(b) temperature of electrolyte

(c) specific gravity of electrolyte

(d) none of the above

11. The storage battery generally used in electric power station is

(a) nickel-cadmium battery

(b) zinc-carbon battery

(c) lead-acid battery

(d) none of the above

12. The output voltage of a charger is

(a) less than the battery voltage

(b) higher than the battery voltage

(c) the same as the battery voltage

(d) none of the above

13. Cells are connected in series in order to

(a) increase the voltage rating

(6) increase the current rating

(c) increase the life of the cells

(d) none of the above

14. Five 2 V cells are connected in parallel. The output voltage is

(a) 1 V

(6) 1.5 V

(c) 1.75 V

(d) 2 V

15. The capacity of a battery is expressed in terms of

(a) current rating

(b) voltage rating

(c) ampere-hour rating

(d) none of the above

16. Duringthe charging and discharging of a nickel-iron cell

(a) corrosive fumes are produced

(b) water is neither formed nor absorbed

(c) nickel hydroxide remains unsplit

(d) its e.m.f. remains constant

17. As compared to constant-current system, the constant-voltage system of charging a lead acid cell has the advantage of

(a) reducing time of charging

(b) increasing cell capacity

(c) both (a) and (b)

(d) avoiding excessive gassing

18. A dead storage battery can be revived by

(a) adding distilled water

(6) adding so-called battery restorer

(c) a dose of H2SO4

(d) none of the above

19. As compared to a lead-acid cell, the efficiency of a nickel-iron cell is less due to its

(a) compactness

(b) lower e.m.f.

(c) small quantity of electrolyte used

(d) higher internal resistance

20. Trickle charging of a storage battery helps to

(a) maintain proper electrolyte level

(b) increase its reserve capacity

(c) prevent sulphation

(d) keep it fresh and fully charged

21. Those substances of the cell which take active part in chemical combination and hence produce electricity during charging or discharging are known as_______materials.

(a) passive

(b) active

(c) redundant

(d) inert

22. In a lead-acid cell dilute sulphuric acid (electrolyte) approximately comprises the following

(a) one part H2O, three parts H2SO4

(b) two parts H2O, two parts H2SO4

(c) three parts H2O, one part H2SO4

(d) all H2S04

23. It is noticed that durum charging

(a) there is a rise in voltage

(b) energy is absorbed by the cell

(c) specific gravity of H2SO4 is increased
(d) all of the above
24. It is noticed that during discharging the following does not happen
(a) both anode and cathode become PbS04
(b) specific gravity of H2SO4 decreases
(c) voltage of the cell decreases
(d) the cell absorbs energy
25. The ampere-hour efficiency of a leadacid cell is normally between
(a) 20 to 30%
(b) 40 to 50%
(c) 60 to 70%
(d) 90 to 95%
26. The watt-hour efficiency of a lead-acid cell varies between
(a) 25 to 35%
(b) 40 to 60%
(c) 70 to 80%
(d) 90 to 95%
27. The capacity of a lead-acid cell is measured in
(a) amperes
(b) ampere-hours
(c) watts
(d) watt-hours
28. The capacity of a lead-acid cell depends on
(a) rate of discharge
(b) temperature
(c) density of electrolyte
(d) all above
29. When the lead-acid cell is fully charged, the electrolyte assumes ______appearance
(a) dull
(b) reddish
(c) bright
(d) milky
30. The e.m.f. of an Edison cell, when fully charged, is nearly
(a) 1.4 V
(b) 1 V
(c) 0.9 V
(d) 0.8 V

31. The internal resistance of an alkali cell is nearly _____ times that of the leadacid cell.
(a) two
(b) three
(c) four
(d) five
32. The average charging voltage for alkali cell is about
(a) 1 V
(b) 1.2 V
(c) 1.7 V
(d) 2.1 V
33. On the average the ampere-hour efficiency of an Edison cell is about
(a) 40%
(b) 60%
(c) 70%
(d) 80%
34. The active material of the positive plates of silver-zinc batteries is
(a) silver oxide
(b) lead oxide
(c) lead
(d) zinc powder
35. Lead-acid cell has a life of nearly charges and discharges
(a) 500
(b) 700
(c) 1000
(d) 1250
36. Life of the Edison cell is at least
(a) five years
(b) seven years
(c) eight years
(d) ten years
37. The internal resistance of a lead-acid cell is that of Edison cell
(a) less than
(b) more than
(c) equal to
(d) none of the above
38. Electrolyte used in an Edison cell is
(a) NaOH

(b) KOH
(c) HC1
(d) HN03
39. Electrolyte used in a lead-acid cell is
(a) NaOH
(b) onlyH2S04
(c) only water
(d) dilute H2SO4
40. Negative plate of an Edison cell is made of
(a) copper
(b) lead
(c) iron
(d) silver oxide
41. The open circuit voltage of any storage cell depends wholly upon
(a) its chemical constituents
(b) on the strength of its electrolyte
(c) its temperature
(d) all above
42. The specific gravity of electrolyte is measured by
(a) manometer
(6) a mechanical gauge
(c) hydrometer
(d) psychrometer
43. When the specific gravity of the electrolyte of a lead-acid cell is reduced to 1.1 to 1.15 the cell is in
(a) charged state
(b) discharged state
(c) both (a) and (b)
(d) active state
44. In _______ system the charging current is intermittently controlled at either a
maximum or minimum value
(a) two rate charge control
(b) trickle charge
(c) floating charge
(d) an equalizing charge
45. Over charging
(a) produces excessive gassing

(b) loosens the active material

(e) increases the temperature resulting in buckling of plates

(d) all above

46. Undercharging

(a) reduces specific gravity of the electrolyte

(b) increases specific gravity of the electrolyte

(c) produces excessive gassing

(d) increases the temperature

47. Internal short circuits are caused by

(a) breakdown of one or more separators

(b) excess accumulation of sediment at the bottom of the cell

(c) both (a) and (b)

(d) none of the above

48. The effect of sulphation is that the internal resistance

(a) increases

(b) decreases

(c) remains same

(d) none of the above

49. Excessive formation of lead sulphate on the surface of the plates happens because of

(a) allowing a battery to stand in discharged condition for a long time

(b) topping up with electrolyte

(c) persistent undercharging

(d) all above

50. The substances which combine together to store electrical energy during the charge are called _______ materials

(a) active

(b) passive

(c) inert

(d) dielectric

18] One micrometer (U] is equal to

A] 01mm

B] 001mm

C] 0001mm

D] 00001mm

19] The caliper meant for measuring the width of a slot is

A] Odd leg caliper

B] Outside caliper

C] Jenny caliper

D] Inside calliper

20] The size of the dividers are specified by the -----------

A] Total length of legs

B] Distance between the points when fully opened

C] Length of legs without points

D] distance between the pivot and the point

21] The instrument used to mark parallel lines, parallel to the datum edge is -

A] jenny caliper

B] Divider

C] Outside calliper

D] Inside calliper

22] Which one of the following is an indirect measuring tool?

A] Outside caliper

B] Vernier calliper

C] Steel rule

D] Outside micrometer

23] For cutting thin tubing, the most suitable pitch of the hacksaw blade is

A] 18mm

B] 14mm

C] 1mm

D] 08mm

24] For cutting solid brass, the most suitable pitch of the hacksaw blade is

A] 18mm

B] 14mm

C] 1mm

D] 08mm

25] A new hacksaw blade after a few strokes becomes loose because of the

A] Stretching of the blade

B] Wing-nut threads being worn out

C] Wrong pitch of the blade

D] Improper selection of the set of saws

26] While cutting small diameter pipes, it is advisable to watch regularly and ensure that

A] The cut is along the curved line

B] More saw teeth are in contract

C] The work is not overheated

D] Proper balancing of hacksaw is maintained

27] The vice clamps are used to

A] Protect hard jaws

B] Clamp the work pieces rigidly

C] Protect the finished surfaces

D] Prevent the movable jaw being filed

28] The reference surface during marking is provided by the

A] Surface gauge

B] Workpiece

C] Drawing of the work

D] Marking table surface

29] The size of an engineer's vice is specified by the

A] Length of the movable jaw

B] Width of the jaws

C] Height of the vice

D] Maximum opening of the jaws

30] The part of the universal surface gauge which helps to draw a parallel line along a datum edge is the

A] Rocker arm

B] Snug

C] Fine adjustment screw

D] Guide pins

31] Scribers are made of

A] Mild steel

B] High carbon steel

C] Brass

D] Cast iron

32] Portion of the hammer used for fixing the handle is

A] Face

B] Peen

C] Cheek

D] Eye hole

33] Weight of the hammer for the marking purpose is

A] 250g

B] 500g

C] 1 kg
D] 2 kgs
34] The size of the dividers are specified by the
A] Total length of the legs
B] Distance between the points when fully opened
C] Length of legs without the points
D] Distance between the pivot and the point
35] The included angle of the groove of 'V' block is always
A] 45◦
B] 60◦
C] 90◦
D] 120◦
36] 'V' blocks are available in grades of
A] A & B
B] A,B & C
C] 1,2 & 3
D] 1 & 2
37] 'V' blocks of grade 'B' are made of
A] Cast iron
B] Mild steel
C] Steel
D] Cast steel
38] Name the punch used to locate the centre
A] Prick punch 30°
B] Prick punch 60°
C] Centre punch
D] Dot punch
39] The point angle of centre punch is --------
A] 30°
B] 50°
c] 900
D] 1200
40] Punches are used for forming ---------of any shape
A] Holes
B] Mining
C] Knurling
D] Reaming
41] Generally the length of the handle of the vice is ---------

A] 15 times the normal size of the vice
B] 25 times the normal size of the vice
C] 35 times the normal size of the vice
D] 45 times the normal size of the vice
42] Bench vice spindle is made of
A] mild steel
B] Cast iron
C] Tool steel
D] Bronze
43] The convexity of files helps
A] To file concave surfaces
B] To file convex surfaces
C] To prevent rounding of edges of work
D] The file to become straight when pressure is applied
44] Which file used for filling wood, leather and other soft material?
A] Single cut file
B] Double cut file
c] Rasp cut file
D] Curved cut file
45] File used is used for ------------
A] Cleaning the work piece
C] Renewing the file teeth
B] cleaning the file teeth
D] Cleaning the chips
46] File card is used to --------
A] Clean the work piece
C] Renew the file teeth
B] Clean the file teeth
47] The point angle of scriber is -----------
A] 30°
B] 60°
C] 5° to 10°
D] 12° to 15°
48] The cutting angle for chipping cast iron is
A] 375◦
B] 55◦
C] 60◦
D] 90◦

49] The chisel will dig into the material when

A] The rake angle is more

B] The clearance angle is too low

C] The angle of inclination is more

D] The angle of inclination is too low

50] A slight convexity is given to the cutting edge to

A] Cut curved surfaces

B] Cut sharp corners

C] Prevent digging of the ends

D] Allow the lubricant to enter

51] Surface plates are made of

A] High grade cast steel

B] Fine-grained cast iron

C] Alloy steels

D] Wrought iron

52] The taper shank drills are held on the machine by means of

A] Chucks

B] Sleeves

C] Drift

D] Vice

53] Drill chucks are fitted on the drilling machine spindle by means of a

A] Knurled ring

B] Arbor

C] Drift

D] Pinion and key

54] The Morse taper provided on drills ranges between

A] MT 1 to MT 5

B] MT 1 to MT 4

C] MT 0 to MT 5

D] MT 0 to MT 4

55] A drift is used for

A] Drawing a drill location

B] Fixing chuck on the machine spindle

C] Removing a broken drill from the work

D] Removing the drill from the machine spindle

56] When the taper shank of the drill is larger than the machine spindle, the device to hold the drill is a

A] Drill sleeve

B] Taper socket

C] Drill drift

D] Chuck and key

57] The suitable cutting fluid for drilling mild steel in a drilling machine is

A] Synthetic soluble oil

B] Neat oil

C] Distilled water

D] Soluble oil

58] A special feature of the radial drilling machine is

A] It can be used for drilling with a HSS drill

B] Table can be moved and set at any position

C] A variety of speeds is available

D] The spindle can be brought to any position

59] The point angle of drills depends on

A] The size of the drill

B] The type of machine

C] The material of the work

D] The RPM of the drill

60] The point angle for a standard drill is

A] 60°

B] 108°

C] 118°

D] 135°

61] The helical angle determines the

A] Cutting angle

B] Chew angle

C] Rake angle

D] Lip angle

62] The clearance angle of the drill is between

A] 3° to 5°

B] 8° to 12°

C] 12° to 20°

D] 15° to 20°

63] In a remote place (no electricity available] a rail track is to be drilled Choose the right drilling machine

A] Radial drilling machine

B] Pillar drilling machine

C] Ratchet drilling machine

D] Sensitive drilling Machine

64] A drilling machine used by a carpenter for cabinet making is a

A] Ratchet drilling machine

B] Radial drilling machine

C] Breast drilling machine

D] Sensitive drilling machine

65] Which one of the following drilling machines is used for drilling holes where electricity is not available?

A] Bench drilling machine

B] Pillar drilling machine

C] Redial drilling machine

D] Ratchet drilling machine

66] Which one of the following drilling machine is used for heavy duty work?

A] Bench drilling machine

B] Pillar drilling machine

C] Radial drilling machine

D] Electric hand drilling machine

67] Drill chuck are held on the machine spindle by means of ------

A] arbor

B] Drift

C] draw-in bar

D] Chuck nut

68] Different speeds are obtained in a sensitive bench drilling machine by ----

A] Belt pulley mechanism

B] Hydraulic mechanism

C] Rack and Pinion mechanism

D] Cam and follower mechanism

69] Tap are re sharpened by grinding -----

A] Hutes

B] Threads

C] Diameter

D] Relief

70] The tapping drill size for M10 x 15 is ----------

A] 82

B] 83

C] 84

D] 85

71] A nut is to be made for a screw of M10XIS What should be the size of drilled hole?

A] 8-5 mm

B] 90 mm

C] 95 mm

D] 100 mm

72] Ribs are given on the unmachined portion of the angle plate for

A] Easy handling

B] Convenience in manufacturing

C] Clamping while setting on machines

D] Rigidity and to prevent distortion

73] The slots on the angle plate are given for

A] Reducing weight

B] Aligning the work

C] Lifting using hooks

D] Accommodating bolts

74] The size of the angle plates is stated by

A] Weight

B] Length

C] Length x width

D] Size number

75] for making gutters, roof flashing, hoods etc

A] Galvanised iron

B] Stainless steel

C] Copper sheet

D] Metal sheets

76] in dairies food processing, kitchen ware etc

A] Galvanised iron

B] Stainless steel

C] Copper sheet

D] Metal sheets

77] for making buckets, heating ducts, cabinets etc

A] Galvanised iron

B] Stainless steel

C] Copper sheet

D] Metal sheets

78] in canneries and chemical plants Metal sheets

A] Galvanised iron

B] Stainless steel

C] Copper sheet

D] Metal sheets

79] Rivets for Joining sheets to thick plates]

A] Countersunk head

B] Flat head

C] Pan head

D] Mushroom

80] Rivets for Joining sheet metal]

A] Countersunk head

B] Flat head

C] Pan head

D] Mushroom

81] Rivets for Heavy fabrication work]

A] Countersunk head

B] Flat head

C] Pan head

D] Mushroom

82] Rivets for Reduces the height of rivet head above the meta\ surface

A] Countersunk head

B] Flat head

C] Pan head

D] Mushroom

83] Rivets for commonly used for structural work]

A] Countersunk head

B] Flat head

C] Pan head

D] Snap head

1. Tesla is a unit of

(a) field strength

(b) inductance

(c) flux density

(d) flux

2. A permeable substance is one

(a) which is a good conductor

(6) which is a bad conductor
(c) which is a strong magnet
(d) through which the magnetic lines of force can pass very easily
3. The materials having low retentivity are suitable for making
(a) weak magnets
(b) temporary magnets
(c) permanent magnets
(d) none of the above
4. A magnetic field exists around
(a) iron
(b) copper
(c) aluminium
(d) moving charges
5. Ferrites are materials.
(a) paramagnetic
(b) diamagnetic
(c) ferromagnetic
(d) none of the above
6. Air gap has________eluctance as compared to iron or steel path
(a) little
(b) lower
(c) higher
(d) zero
7. The direction of magnetic lines of force is
(a) from south pole to north pole
(b) from north pole to south pole
(c) from one end of the magnet to another
(d) none of the above
8. Which of the following is a vector quantity ?
(a) Relative permeability
(b) Magnetic field intensity
(c) Flux density
(d) Magnetic potential
9. The two conductors of a transmission line carry equal current I in opposite
directions. The force on each conductor is
(a) proportional to 7
(b) proportional to X

(c) proportional to distance between the conductors

(d) inversely proportional to I

10. A material which is slightly repelled by a magnetic field is known as

(a) ferromagnetic material

(b) diamagnetic material

(c) paramagnetic material

(d) conducting material

11. When an iron piece is placed in a magnetic field

(a) the magnetic lines of force will bend away from their usual paths in order to go

away from the piece

(b) the magnetic lines of force will bend away from their usual paths in order to

pass through the piece

(c) the magnetic field will not be affected

(d) the iron piece will break

12. Fleming's left hand rule is used to find

(a) direction of magnetic field due to current carrying conductor

(b) direction of flux in a solenoid

(c) direction of force on a current carrying conductor in a magnetic field

(d) polarity of a magnetic pole

13. The ratio of intensity of magnetisation to the magnetisation force is known as

(a) flux density

(b) susceptibility

(c) relative permeability

(d) none of the above

14. Magnetising steel is normals difficult because

(a) it corrodes easily

(6) it has high permeability

(c) it has high specific gravity

(d) it has low permeability

15. The left hand rule correlates to

(a) current, induced e.m.f. and direction of force on a conductor

(b) magnetic field, electric field and direction of force on a conductor

(c) self induction, mutual induction and direction of force on a conductor

(d) current, magnetic field and direction of force on a conductor

16. The unit of relative permeability is

(a) henry/metre

(b) henry

(c) henry/sq. m

(d) it is dimensionless

17. A conductor of length L has current I passing through it, when it is placed

parallel to a magnetic field. The force experienced by the conductor will be

(a) zero

(b) BLI

(c) B2LI

(d) BLI2

18. The force between two long parallel conductors is inversely proportional to

(a) radius of conductors

(b) current in one conductor

(c) product of current in two conductors

(d) distance between the conductors

19. Materials subjected to rapid reversal of magnetism should have

(a) large area oiB-H loop

(b) high permeability and low hysteresis loss

(c) high co-ercivity and high retentivity

(d) high co-ercivity and low density

20. Indicate which of the following material does not retain magnetism permanently.

(a) Soft iron

(b) Stainless steel

(e) Hardened steel

(d) None of the above

21. The main constituent of permalloy is

(a) cobalt

(b) chromium

(c) nickel

(d) tungsten

22. The use of permanent magnets is. not made in

(a) magnetoes

(6) energy meters

(c) transformers
(d) loud-speakers
23. Paramagnetic materials have relative permeability
(a) slightly less than unity
(b) equal to unity
(c) slightly more than unity
(d) equal to that ferromagnetic mate rials
25. Substances which have permeability less than the permeability of free space
are known as
(a) ferromagnetic
(b) paramagnetic
(c) diamagnetic
(d) bipolar
27. In the left hand rule, forefinger always represents
(a) voltage
(b) current
(c) magnetic field
(d) direction of force on the conductor
28. Which of the following is a ferromagnetic material ?
(a) Tungsten
(b) Aluminium
(c) Copper
(d) Nickel
29. Ferrites are a sub-group of
(a) non-magnetic materials
(6) ferro-magnetic materials
(c) paramagnetic materials
(d) ferri-magnetic materials
30. Gilbert is a unit of
(a) electromotive force
(b) magnetomotive force
(c) conductance
(d) permittivity
51. Unit for quantity of electricity is
(a) ampere-hour
(b) watt
(c) joule

(d) coulomb

52. The Biot-savart's law is a general modification of

(a) Kirchhoffs law

(b) Lenz's law

(c) Ampere's law

(d) Faraday's laws

53. The most effective and quickest may of making a magnet from soft iron is by

(a) placing it inside a coil carrying current

(b) induction

(c) the use of permanent magnet

(d) rubbing with another magnet

54. The commonly used material for shielding or screening magnetism is

(a) copper

(b) aluminium

(c) soft iron

(d) brass

55. If a copper disc is rotated rapidly below a freely suspended magnetic needle,

the magnetic needle shall start rotating with a velocity

(a) less than that of disc but in opposite direction

(b) equal to that of disc and in the same direction

(c) equal to that of disc and in the opposite direction

(d) less than that of disc and in the same direction

56. A permanent magnet

(a) attracts somc substances and repels others

(b) attracts all paramagnetic substances and repels others

(c) attracts only ferromagnetic substances

(d) attracts ferromagnetic substances and repels all others

57. The retentivity (a property) of material is useful for the construction of

(a) permanent magnets

(b) transformers

(c) non-magnetic substances

(d) electromagnets

58. The relative permeability of materials is not constant.

(a) diamagnetic

(b) paramagnetic

(c) ferromagnetic

(d) insulating

59. The materials are a bit inferior conductors of magnetic flux than air.

(a) ferromagnetic

(b) paramagnetic

(c) diamagnetic

(d) dielectric

60. Hysteresis loop in case of magnetically hard materials is more in shape as

compared to magnetically soft materials.

(a) circular

(b) triangular

(c) rectangular

(d) none of the above

61. A rectangular magnet of magnetic moment M is cut into two piece of same

length, the magnetic moment of each piece will be

(a) M

(b) M/2

(c) 2 M

(d) M/4

62. A keeper is used to

(a) change the direction of magnetic lines

(b) amplify flux

(c) restore lost flux

(d) provide a closed path for flux

63. Magnetic moment is a

(a) pole strength

(6) universal constant

(c) scalar quantity

(d) vector quantity

64. The change of cross-sectional area of conductor in magnetic field will affect

(a) reluctance of conductor

(b) resistance of conductor

(c) (a) and (b) both in the same way

(d) none of the above

65. The uniform magnetic field is

(a) the field of a set of parallel conductors

(b) the field of a single conductor

(c) the field in which all lines of magnetic flux are parallel and equidistant

(d) none of the above

66. The magneto-motive force is

(a) the voltage across the two ends of exciting coil

(b) the flow of an electric current

(c) the sum of all currents embraced by one line of magnetic field

(d) the passage of magnetic field through an exciting coil

91. For which of the following materials the saturation value is the highest ?

(a) Ferromagnetic materials

(6) Paramagnetic materials

(c) Diamagnetic materials

(d) Ferrites

92. The magnetic materials exhibit the property of magnetisation because of

(a) orbital motion of electrons

(b) spin of electrons

(c) spin of nucleus

(d) either of these

93. For which of the following materials the net magnetic moment should be zero ?

(a) Diamagnetic materials

(b) Ferrimagnetic materials

(c) Antiferromagnetic materials

(d) Antiferrimagnetic materials

94. The attraction capacity of electromagnet will increase if the

(a) core length increases i

(b) core area increases

(c) flux density decreases

(d) flux density increases

95. Which of the following statements is correct ?

(a) The conductivity of ferrites is better than ferromagnetic materials

(b) The conductivity of ferromagnetic materials is better than ferrites

(c) The conductivity of ferrites is very high

(d) The conductivity of ferrites is same as that of ferromagnetic materials

96. Temporary magnets are used in

(a) loud-speakers

(b) generators

(c) motors

(d) <u>all of the above</u>

97. Main causes of noisy solenoid are

(a) strong tendency of fan out of laminations at the end caused by repulsion

among magnetic lines of force

(b) uneven bearing surface, caused by dirt or uneven wear between moving and

stationary parts

(c) <u>both of above</u>

(d) none of the above

99. Core of an electromagnet should have

(a) low coercivity

(6) high susceptibility

(c) <u>both of the above</u>

(d) none of the above

100. Magnetism of a magnet can be destroyed by

(a) heating

(b) hammering

(c) by inductive action of another magnet

(d) <u>by all above methods</u>

1. A semiconductor is formed by .... bonds.

A] <u>Covalent</u>

B] Electrovalent

C] Co-ordinate

D] None of the above

2. A semiconductor has .... temperature coefficient of resistance.

A] Positive

B] Zero

C] <u>Negative</u>

D] None of the above

3. The most commonly used semiconductor is ....

A] Germanium

B] Silicon

C] Carbon

D] Sulphur

6. The resistivity of a pure silicon is about ....

A] 100 O cm

B] 6000 O cm

C] 3 x 105 O m

D] 6 x 10-8 O cm

7. When a pure semiconductor is heated, its resistance ....

A] Goes up

B] Goes down

C] Remains the same

D] Can't say

8. The strength of a semiconductor crystal comes from ....

A] Forces between nuclei

B] Forces between protons

C] Electron-pair bonds

D] None of the above

9. When a pentavalent impurity is added to a pure semiconductor, it becomes ....

A] An insulator

B] An intrinsic semiconductor

C] p-type semiconductor

D] n-type semiconductor

10. Addition of pentavalent impurity to a semiconductor createsmany ....

A] Free electrons

B] Holes

C] Valence electrons

D] Bound electrons

11. A pentavalent impurity has .... Valence electrons

A] 35

B] 4

C] 6

12. An n-type semiconductor is ....

A] Positively charged

B] Negatively charged

C] Electrically neutral

D] None of the above

14. Addition of trivalent impurity to a semiconductor creates many ....

A] Holes

B] Free electrons

C] Valence electrons

D] Bound electrons

15. A hole in a semiconductor is defined as ....

A] A free electron

B] The incomplete part of an electron pair bond

C] A free proton

D] A free neutron

16. The impurity level in an extrinsic semiconductor is about ..... of pure semiconductor.

A] 10 atoms for 108 atoms

B] 1 atom for 108 atoms

C] 1 atom for 104 atoms

D] 1 atom for 100 atoms

17. As the doping to a pure semiconductor increases, the bulk resistance of the semiconductor ....

A] Remains the same

B] Increases

C] Decreases

D] None of the above

18. A hole and electron in close proximity would tend to ....

A] Repel each other

B] Attract each other

C] Have no effect on each other

D] None of the above

19. In a semiconductor, current conduction is due to ....

A] Only holes

B] Only free electrons

C] Holes and free electrons

D] None of the above

20. The random motion of holes and free electrons due to thermal agitation is called ....

A] Diffusion

B] Pressure

C] Ionisation

D] None of the above

21. A forward biased pn junction diode has a resistance of the order of

A] Ok

B] O

C] MO

D] None of the above

22. The battery connections required to forward bias a pn junction are ......

A] +ve terminal to p and –ve terminal to n

B] -ve terminal to p and +ve terminal to n

C] -ve terminal to p and –ve terminal to n

D] None of the above

23. The barrier voltage at a pn junction for germanium is about ....

A] 5 V

B] 3 V

C] Zero

D] 3 V

24. In the depletion region of a pn junction, there is a shortage of ....

A] Acceptor ions

B] Holes and electrons

C] Donor ions

D] None of the above

25. A reverse bias pn junction has ....

A] narrow depletion layer

B] Almost no current

C] Very low resistance

D] Large current flow

26. A pn junction acts as a ....

A] Controlled switch

B] Bidirectional switch

C] Unidirectional switch

D] None of the above

27. A reverse biased pn junction has resistance of the order of

A] Ok

B] O

C] MO

D] None of the above

28. The leakage current across a pn junction is due to ....

A] Minority carriers
B] Majority carriers
C] Junction capacitance
D] None of the above

29. When the temperature of an extrinsic semiconductor is increased, the pronounced effect is on......
A] Junction capacitance
B] Minority carriers
C] Majority carriers
D] None of the above

30. With forward bias to a pn junction , the width of depletion layer ....
A] Decreases
B] Increases
C] Remains the same
D] None of the above

31. The leakage current in a pn junction is of the order of
A] Aa
B] mA
C] kA
D] μA

32. In an intrinsic semiconductor, the number of free electrons ....
A] Equals the number of holes
B] Is greater than the number of holes
C] Is less than the number of holes
D] None of the above

33. At room temperature, an intrinsic semiconductor has ....
A] Many holes only
B] A few free electrons and holes
C] Many free electrons only
D] No holes or free electrons

34. At absolute temperature, an intrinsic semiconductor has ....
A] A few free electrons
B] Many holes
C] Many free electrons
D] No holes or free electrons

35. At room temperature, an intrinsic silicon crystal acts approximately as ......
A] A battery

B] A conductor
C] <u>An insulator</u>
D] A piece of copper wire
1. A crystal diode has ....
one pn junction
two pn junctions
three pn junctions
none of the above
ANS: 1
2. A crystal diode has forward resistance of the order of ....
kΩ
Ω
MΩ
none of the above
ANS: 2
3. If the arrow of crystal diode symbol is positive w.r.t. bar, then diode is .... biased.
forward
reverse
either forward or reverse
none of the above
ANS: 1
SEMICONDUCTOR DIODE
Questions and Answers pdf
4. The reverse current in a diode is of the order of ....
kA
mA
μA
A
ANS: 3
5. The forward voltage drop across a silicon diode is about ....
2.5 V
3 V
10 V
0.7 V
ANS: 4

6. A crystal diode is used as ....
an amplifier
a rectifier
an oscillator
a voltage regulator
ANS: 2
7. The d.c. resistance of a crystal diode is .... its a.c. resistance
the same as
more than
less than
none of the above
ANS: 3
8. An ideal crystal diode is one which behaves as a perfect .... when forward biased.
conductor
insulator
resistance material
none of the above
ANS: 1
9. The ratio of reverse resistance and forward resistance of a germanium crystal diode is about ....
1 : 1
100 : 1
1000 : 1
40,000 : 1
ANS: 4
10. The leakage current in a crystal diode is due to ....
minority carriers
majority carriers
junction capacitance
none of the above
ANS: 1
11. If the temperature of a crystal diode increases, then leakage current ....
remains the same
decreases
increases
becomes zero

ANS: 3

12. The PIV rating of a crystal diode is .... that of equivalent vacuum diode

the same as

lower than

more than

none of the above

ANS: 2

13. If the doping level of a crystal diode is increased, the breakdown voltage.............

remains the same

is increased

is decreased

none of the above

ANS: 3

14. The knee voltage of a crystal diode is approximately equal to ....

applied voltage

breakdown voltage

forward voltage

barrier potential

ANS: 4

15. When the graph between current through and voltage across a device is a straight line, the device is referred to as ....

linear

active

nonlinear

passive

ANS: 1

16. When the crystal current diode current is large, the bias is ....

forward

inverse

poor

reverse

ANS: 1

17. A crystal diode is a .... device

non-linear

bilateral

linear
none of the above
ANS: 1
18. A crystal diode utilises .... characteristic for rectification
reverse
forward
forward or reverse
none of the above
ANS: 2
19. When a crystal diode is used as a rectifier, the most important consideration is ....
forward characteristic
doping level
reverse characteristic
PIC rating
ANS: 4
20. If the doping level in a crystal diode is increased, the width of depletion layer...........
remains the same
is decreased
in increased
none of the above
ANS: 3
21. A zener diode has ....
one pn junction
two pn junctions
three pn junctions
none of the above
ANS: 1
22. A zener diode is used as ....
an amplifier
a voltage regulator
a rectifier
a multivibrator
ANS: 2
23. The doping level in a zener diode is .... that of a crystal diode
the same as
less than

more than
none of the above
ANS: 3
24. A zener diode is always .... connected.
reverse
forward
either reverse or forward
none of the above
ANS: 1
25. A zener diode utilizes .... characteristics for its operation.
forward
reverse
both forward and reverse
none of the above
ANS: 2
26. In the breakdown region, a zener didoe behaves like a .... source.
constant voltage
constant current
constant resistance
none of the above
ANS: 1
27. A zener diode is destroyed if it.............
is forward biased
is reverse biased
carrier more than rated current
nonc of the above
ANS: 3
28. A series resistance is connected in the zener circuit to...........
properly reverse bias the zener
protect the zener
properly forward bias the zener
none of the above
ANS: 2
29. A zener diode is .... device
a non-linear
a linear
an amplifying

none of the above

ANS: 1

30. A zener diode has .... breakdown voltage

undefined

sharp

zero

none of the above

ANS: 2

31. .... rectifier has the lowest forward resistance

solid state

vacuum tube

gas tube

none of the above

ANS: 1

32. Mains a.c. power is converrted into d.c. power for ....

lighting purposes

heaters

using in electronic equipment

none of the above

ANS: 3

33. The disadvantage of a half-wave rectifier is that the..................

components are expensive

diodes must have a higher power rating

output is difficult to filter

none of the above

ANS: 3

34. If the a.c. input to a half-wave rectifier is an r.m.s value of 400/√2 volts, then diode PIV rating is ....

400/√2 V

400 V

400 x √2 V

none of the above

ANS: 2

35. The ripple factor of a half-wave rectifier is ....

21

.21

2.5

0.48

ANS: 4

36. There is a need of transformer for ....

half-wave rectifier

centre-tap full-wave rectifier

bridge full-wave rectifier

none of the above

ANS: 2

37. The PIV rating of each diode in a bridge rectifier is .... that of the equivalent centre-tap rectifier

one-half

the same as

twice

four times

ANS: 1

38. For the same secondary voltage, the output voltage from a centretap rectifier is .... than that of bridge rectifier

twice

thrice

four time

one-half

ANS: 4

39. If the PIV rating of a diodc is exceeded, ...

the diode conducts poorly

the diode is destroyed

the diode behaves like a zener diode

none of the above

ANS: 2

40. A 10 V power supply would use .... as filter capacitor.

paper capacitor

mica capacitor

electrolytic capacitor

air capacitor

ANS: 3

41. A 1,000 V power supply would use .... as a filter capacitor

paper capacitor

air capacitor

mica capacitor

electrolytic capacitor

ANS: 1

42. The .... filter circuit results in the best voltage regulation

choke input

capacitor input

resistance input

none of the above

ANS: 1

43. A half-wave rectifier has an input voltage of 240 V r.m.s. If the step-down transformer has a turns ratio of 8:1, what is the peak load voltage? Ignore diode drop.

27.5 V

86.5 V

30 V

42.5 V

ANS: 4

44. The maximum efficiency of a half-wave rectifier is ....

40.6 %

81.2 %

50 %

25 %

ANS: 1

45. The most widely used rectifier is ....

half-wave rectifier

centre-tap full-wave rectifier

bridge full-wave rectifier

none of the above

ANS:3

1. Which of the following are the applications of D.C. system ?

(a) Battery charging work

(b) Arc welding

(c) Electrolytic and electro-chemical processes

(d) Arc lamps for search lights

(e) All of the above

Ans: e

2. Which of the following methods may be used to convert A.C. system to D.C. ?

(a) Rectifiers

(b) Motor converters

(c) Motor-generator sets
(d) Rotary converters
(e) All of the above
Ans: e
3. In a single phase rotary converter the number of slip rings will be
(a) two
(b) three
(c) four
(d) six
(e) none
Ans: a
4. A synchronous converter can be started
(a) by means of a small auxiliary motor
(b) from AC. side as induction motor
(c) from D.C. side as D.C. motor
(d) any of the above methods
(e) none of the above methods
Ans: d
5. A rotary converter is a single machine with
(a) one armature and one field
(b) two armatures and one field
(c) one armature and two fields
(d) none of the above
Ans: a
6. A rotary converter combines the function of
(a) an induction motor and a D.C. generator
(b) a synchronous motor and a D.C. generator.
(c) a D.C. series motor and a D.C. generator
(d) none of the above
Ans: b
7. Which of the following is reversible in action ?
(a) Motor generator set
(b) Motor converter
(c) Rotary converter
(d) Any of the above
(e) None of the above
Ans: c

8. Which of the following metals is generally manufactured by electrolysis

process ?

(a) Load

(b) Aluminium

(c) Copper

(d) Zinc

(e) None of the above

Ans: b

9. With a motor converter it is possible to obtain D.C. voltage only upto

(a) 200-100 V

(6) 600—800 V

(c) 1000—1200 V

(d) 1700—2000 V

Ans: d

10. Normally, which of the following is used, when a large-scale conversion from

AC. to D.C. power is required ?

(a) Motor-generator set

(b) Motor converter

(c) Rotary converter

(d) Mercury arc rectifier

Ans: d

11. A rotary converter in general construction and design, is more or less like

(a) a transformer

(b) an induction motor

(c) an alternator

(d) any D.C. machine

Ans: d

12. A rotary converter operates at a

(a) low power factor

(6) high power factor

(c) zero power factor

(d) none of the above

Ans: b

13. In which of the following appUcations, direct current is absolutely essential ?

(a) Illumination
(b) Electrolysis
(c) Variable speed operation
(d) Traction
Ans: b

14. Which of the following AC. motors is usually used in large motor-generator
sets?
(a) Synchronous motor
(b) Squirrel cage induction motor
(c) Slip ring induction motor
(d) Any of the above
Ans: a

15. In a rotary converter armature currents are
(a) d.c. only
(b) a.c. only
(c) partly a.c. and partly d.c.
Ans: c

16. In which of the following equipment direct current is needed ?
(a) Telephones
(b) Relays
(c) Time switches
(d) All of the above
Ans: d

17. In a rotary converter I2R losses as compared to a D.C. generator of the same
size will be
(a) same
(b) less
(c) double
(d) three times
Ans: b

18. In a mercury arc rectifier positive ions are attracted towards
(a) anode
(b) cathode
(c) shell bottom
(d) mercury pool
Ans: b

19. Mercury, in arc rectifiers, is chosen for cathode because
(a) its ionization potential is relatively low
(b) its atomic weight is quite high
(c) its boiling point and specific heat are low
(d) it remains in liquid state at ordi¬nary temperature
(e) all of the above
Ans: e
20. The ionization potential of mercury is approximately
(a) 5.4 V
(b) 8.4 V
(c) 10.4 V
(d) 16.4 V
Ans: c
21. The potential drop in the arc, in a mercury arc rectifier, varies
(a) 0.05 V to 0.2 V per cm length of the arc
(b) 0.5 V to 1.5 V per cm length of the arc
(c) 2 V to 3.5 V per cm length of the arc
(d) none of the above
Ans: d
22. The voltage drop between the anode and cathode, of a mercury arc rectifier
comprises of the following
(a) anode drop and cathode drop
(b) anode drop and arc drop
(c) cathode drop and arc drop
(d) anode drop, cathode drop and arc drop
Ans: d
23. Glass rectifiers are usually made into units capable of D.C. output (maximum
continuous rating) of
(a) 100 A at 100 V
(b) 200 A at 200 V
(c) 300 A at 300 V
(d) 400 A at 400 V
(e) 500 A at 500 V
Ans: e
24. The voltage drop at anode, in a mercury arc rectifier is due to
(a) self restoring property of mercury

(b) high ionization potential
(c) energy spent in overcoming the electrostatic field
(d) high temperature inside the rectifier
Ans: c

25. The internal efficiency of a mercury arc rectifier depends on
(a) voltage only
(b) current only
(c) voltage and current
(d) r.m.s. value of current
(e) none of the above
Ans: a

26. If cathode and anode connections in a mercury arc rectifier are inter changed
(a) the rectifier will not operate
(b) internal losses will be reduced
(c) both ion and electron streams will move in the same direction
(d) the rectifier will operate at reduced efficiency
Ans: a

27. The cathdde voltage drop, in a mercury arc rectifier, is due to
(a) expenditure of energy in ionization
(b) surface resistance
(c) expenditure of energy in overcoming the electrostatic field
(d) expenditure of energy in liberating electrons from the mercury
Ans: d

28. To produce cathode spot in a mercury arc rectifier
(a) anode is heated
(b) tube is evacuated
(c) an auxiliary electrode is used
(d) low mercury vapour pressures are used
Ans: c

29. The advantage of mercury arc rectifier is that
(a) it is light in weight and occupies small floor space
(b) it has high efficiency
(c) it has high overload capacity
(d) it is comparatively noiseless
(e) all of the above
Ans: e

30. In a mercury pool rectifier, the voltage drop across its electrodes

(a) is directly proportional to load
(b) is inversely proportional to load
(c) varies exponentially with the load current
(d) is almost independent of load current
Ans: d

RECTIFIERS & CONVERTERS – Electrical Engineering Interview Questions
and Answers

31. In a three-phase mercury arc rectifiers each anode conducts for
(a) one-third of a cycle
(b) one-fourth of a cycle
(c) one-half a cycle
(d) two-third of a cycle
Ans: a

32. In a mercury arc rectifier characteristic blue luminosity is due to
(a) colour of mercury
(b) ionization
(c) high temperature
(d) electron streams
Ans: b

33. Which of the following mercury arc rectifier will deliver least undulating
current?
(a) Six-phase
(b) Three-phase
(c) Two-phase
(d) Single-phase
Ans: a

34. In a glass bulb mercury arc rectifier the maximum current rating is restricted
to
(a) 2000 A
(b) 1500 A
(c) 1000 A
(d) 500 A
Ans: d

35. In a mercury arc rectifier______ flow from anode to cathode
(a) ions

(b) electrons

(c) ions and electrons

(d) any of the above

Ans: a

36. When a rectifier is loaded which of the following voltage drops take place ?

(a) Voltage drop in transformer reactance

(6) Voltage drop in resistance of transformer and smoothing chokes

(c) Arc voltage drop

(d) All of the above

Ans: d

37. On which of the following factors the number of phases for which a rectifier

should be designed depend ?

(a) The voltage regulation of the rec¬tifier should be low

(b) In the output circuit there should be no harmonics

(c) The power factor of the system should be high

(d) The rectifier supply transformer should be utilized to the best advantage

(e) all of the above

Ans: e

38. A mercury arc rectifier possesses ________ regulation characteristics

(a) straight line

(b) curved line

(c) exponential

(d) none of the above

Ans: d

39. It is the________of the transformer on which the magnitude of angle of

overlap depends.

(a) resistance

(b) capacitance

(c) leakage reactance

(d) any of the above

Ans: c

41. In a grid control of mercury arc rectifiers when the grid is made positive

relative to cathode, then it the electrons on their may to anode.

(a) accelerates

(b) decelerates

(c) any of the above

(d) none of the above

Ans: a

42. In mercury arc rectifiers having grid, the arc can be struck between anode and

cathode only when the grid attains a certain potential, this potential being known

as

(a) maximum grid voltage

(b) critical grid voltage

(c) any of the above

(d) none of the above

Ans: b

43. In phase-shift control method the control is carried out by varying the of grid

voltage.

(a) magnitude

(b) polarity

(c) phase

(d) any of the above

(e) none of the above

Ans: c

16.44. In a phase-shift control method, the phase shift between anode and grid

voltages can be achieved by means of

(a) shunt motor

(6) synchronous motor

(c) induction regulator

(d) synchronous generator

Ans: c

45. The metal rectifiers are preferred to valve rectifiers due to which of the

following advantages ?

(a) They are mechanically strong

(b) They do not require any voltage for filament heating

(c) Both (a) and (b)
(d) None of the above
Ans: c
46. Which of the following statement is incorrect ?
(a) Copper oxide rectifier is a linear device
(b) Copper oxide rectifier is not a perfect rectifier
(c) Copper oxide rectifier has a low efficiency
(d) Copper oxide rectifier finds use in control circuits
(e) Copper oxide rectifier is not stable during early life
Ans: a
47. The efficiency of the copper oxide rectifier seldom exceeds
(a) 90 to 95%
(b) 85 to 90%
(c) 80 to 85%
(d) 65 to 75%
Ans: d
48. Copper oxide rectifier is usually designed not to operate above
(a) 10°C
(b) 20°C
(c) 30°C
(d) 45°C
Ans: d
49. Selenium rectifier can be operated at temperatures as high as
(a) 25°C
(b) 40°C
(c) 60°C
(d) 75°C
Ans: d
50. In selenium rectifiers efficiencies ranging from ______ to ______ percent
are attainable
(a) 25, 35
(b) 40, 50
(c) 60, 70
(d) 75, 85
Ans: d
51. Ageing of a selenium rectifier may change the output voltage by
(a) 5 to 10 per cent

(b) 15 to 20 per cent

(c) 25 to 30 per cent

(d) none of the above

Ans: a

52. The applications of selenium rectifiers are usually limited to potential of

(a) 10 V

(b) 30 V

(c) 60 V

(d) 100 V

(e) 200 V

Ans: d

53. Which of the following rectifiers have been used extensively in supplying

direct current for electroplating ?

(a) Copper oxide rectifiers

(b) Selenium rectifiers

(c) Mercury arc rectifiers

(d) Mechanical rectifiers

(e) None of the above

Ans: b

54. A commutating rectifier consists of commutator driven by

(a) an induction motor

(b) a synchronous motor

(c) a D.C. series motor

(d) a D.C. shunt motor

Ans: b

55. Which of the following rectifiers are primarily used for charging of low voltage

batteries from AC. supply ?

(a) Mechanical rectifiers

(b) Copper oxide rectifiers

(c) Selenium rectifiers

(d) Electrolytic rectifiers

(e) Mercury arc rectifiers

Ans: d

56. The efficiency of an electrolytic rectifier is nearly

(a) 80%

(b) 70%

(c) 60%

(d) 40%

Ans: c

57. Which of the following is the loss within the mercury arc rectifier chamber ?

(a) Voltage drop in arc

(6) Voltage drop at the anode

(c) Voltage drop at the cathode

(d) All of the above

Ans: d

58. The metal rectifiers, as compared to mercury arc rectifiers

(a) operate on low temperatures

(b) can operate on high voltages

(c) can operate on heavy loads

(d) give poor regulation

(e) none of the above

Ans: a

59. In a mercury arc rectifier, the anode is usually made of

(a) copper

(b) aluminium

(c) silver

(d) graphite

(e) tungsten

Ans: d

60. Short-circuit test on an induction motor cannot be used to determine

(a) windage losses

(b) copper losses

(c) transformation ratio

(d) power scale of circle diagram

61. In a three-phase induction motor

(a) iron losses in stator will be negligible as compared to that in rotor

(6) iron losses in motor will be neg¬ligible as compared to that in rotor

(c) iron losses in stator will be less than that in rotor

(d) iron losses in stator will be more than that in rotor

62. In case of 3-phase induction motors, plugging means

(a) pulling the motor directly on line without a starter

(b) locking of rotor due to harmonics

(c) starting the motor on load which is more than the rated load

(d) interchanging two supply phases for quick stopping

63. Which is of the following data is required to draw the circle diagram for an induction motor ?

(a) Block rotor test only

(b) No load test only

(c) Block rotor test and no-load test

(d) Block rotor test, no-load test and stator resistance test

64. In three-phase induction motors sometimes copper bars are placed deep in the rotor to

(a) improve starting torque

(b) reduce copper losses

(c) improve efficiency

(d) improve power factor

65. In a three-phase induction motor

(a) power factor at starting is high as compared to that while running

(b) power factor at starting is low as compared to that while running

(c) power factor at starting in the same as that while running

66. The vafcie of transformation ratio of an induction motor can be found by

(a) open-circuit test only

(b) short-circuit test only

(c) stator resistance test

(d) none of the above

67. The power scale of circle diagram of an induction motor can be found from

(a) stator resistance test

(b) no-load test only

(c) short-circuit test only

(d) noue of the above

68. The shape of the torque/slip curve of induction motor is

(a) parabola

(b) hyperbola

(c) rectangular parabola

(d) straigth line

69. A change of 4% of supply voltage to an induction motor will produce a change of appromimately

(a) 4% in the rotor torque

(b) 8% in the rotor torque

(c) 12% in the rotor torque

(d) 16% in the rotor torque

70. The stating torque of the slip ring induction motor can be increased by adding

(a) external inductance to the rotor

(b) external resistance to the rotor

(c) external capacitance to the rotor

(d) both resistance and inductance to rotor

71. A 500 kW, 3-phase, 440 volts, 50 Hz, A.C. induction motor has a speed of 960 r.p.m. on full load. The machine has 6 poles. The slip of the machine will be

(a) 0.01

(b) 0.02

(c) 0.03

(d) 0.04

72. The complete circle diagram of induetion motor can be drawn with the help of

data found from

(a) noload test

(6) blocked rotor test

(c) stator resistance test

(d) all of the above

73. In the squirrel-cage induction motor the rotor slots are usually given slight skew

(a) to reduce the magnetic hum and locking tendency of the rotor

(b) to increase the tensile strength of the rotor bars

(c) to ensure easy fabrication

(d) none of the above

74. The torque of a rotor in an induction motor under running condition is maximum

(a) at the unit value of slip

(b) at the zero value of slip

(c) at the value of the slip which makes rotor reactance per phase equal to the resistance per phase

(d) at the value of the slip which makes the rotor reactance half of the rotor

75. What will happen if the relative speed between the rotating flux of stator and rotor of the induction motor is zero ?

(a) The slip of the motor will be 5%

(b) The rotor will not run

(c) The rotor will run at very high speed

(d) The torque produced will be very large

76. The circle diagram for an induction motor cannot be used to determine

(a) efficiency

(b) power factor

(c) frequency

(d) output

77. Blocked rotor test on induction motors is used to find out

(a) leakage reactance

(b) power factor on short circuit

(c) short-circuit current under rated voltage

(d) all of the above

78. Lubricant used for ball bearing is usually

(a) graphite

(b) grease

(c) mineral oil

(d) molasses

79. An induction motor can run at synchronous speed when

(a) it is run on load

(b) it is run in reverse direction

(c) it is run on voltage higher than the rated voltage

(d) e.m.f. is injected in the rotor circuit

80. Which motor is preferred for use in mines where explosive gases exist ?

(a) Air motor

(b) Induction motor

(c) D.C. shunt motor

(d) Synchronous motor

81. The torque developed by a 3-phase induction motor least depends on

(a) rotor current

(b) rotor power factor

(c) rotor e.m.f.

(d) shaft diameter

82. In an induction motor if air-gap is increased
(a) the power factor will be low
(b) windage losses will be more
(c) bearing friction will reduce
(d) copper loss will reduce In an induction motor
83. In induction motor, percentage slip depends on
(a) supply frequency
(b) supply voltage
(c) copper losses in motor
(d) none of the above
85. In case of a double cage induction motor, the inner cage has
(a) high inductance arid low resistance
(b) low inductance and high resistance
(c) low inductance and low resistance
(d) high inductance and high resistance
86. The low power factor of induction motor is due to
(a) rotor leakage reactance
(b) stator reactance
(c) the reactive lagging magnetizing current necessary to generate the magnetic flux
(d) all of the above
87. Insertion of reactance in the rotor circuit
(a) reduces starting torque as well as maximum torque
(b) increases starting torque as well as maximum torque
(c) increases starting torque but maxi-mum torque remains unchanged
(d) increases starting torque but maxi-mum torque decreases
88. Insertion of resistance in the rotcir of an induction motor to develop a given torque
(a) decreases the rotor current
(b) increases the rotor current
(c) rotor current becomes zero
(d) rotor current rernains same
89. For driving high inertia loods best type of induction motor suggested is
(a) slip ring type
(b) squirrel cage type
(c) any of the above
(d) none of the above

90. Temperature of the stator winding of a three phase induction motor is

obtained by

(a) resistance rise method

(b) thermometer method

(c) embedded temperature method

(d) all above methods

91. The purpose of using short-circuit gear is

(a) to short circuit the rotor at slip rings

(b) to short circuit the starting resistances in the starter

(c) to short circuit the stator phase of motor to form star

(d) none of the above

92. In a squirrel cage motor the induced e.m.f. is

(a) dependent on the shaft loading

(b) dependent on the number of slots

(c) slip times the stand still e.m.f. induced in the rotor

(d) none of the above

93. Less maintenance troubles are experienced in case of

(a) slip ring induction motor

(b) squirrel cage induction motor

(c) both (a) and (b)

(d) none of the above

94. A squirrel cage induction motor is not selected when

(a) initial cost is the main consideration

(b) maintenance cost is to be kept low

(c) higher starting torque is the main consideration

(d) all above considerations are involved

95. Reduced voltage starter can be used with

(a) slip ring motor only but not with squirrel cage induction motor

(b) squirrel cage induction motor only but not with slip ring motor

(c) squirrel cage as well as slip ring induction motor

(d) none of the above

96. Slip ring motor is preferred over squirrel cage induction motor where

(a) high starting torque is required

(b) load torque is heavy

(c) heavy pull out torque is required

(d) all of the above

97. In a star-delta starter of an induction motor

(a) resistance is inserted in the stator

(b) reduced voltage is applied to the stator

(c) resistance is inserted in the rotor

(d) applied voltage perl stator phase is 57.7% of the line voltage

98. The torque of an induction motor is

(a) directly proportional to slip

(b) inversely proportional to slip

(c) proportional to the square of the slip

(d) none of the above

99. The rotor of an induction motor runs at

(a) synchronous speed

(b) below synchronous speed

(c) above synchronous speed

(d) any of the above

100. The starting torque of a three phase induction motor can be increased by

(a) increasing slip

(b) increasing current

(c) both (a) and (b)

(d) none of the above

Q.1. Which of the following is the biggest unit of memory?

A] Gigabytes.

B] bytes.

C] Megabytes.

D] Kilobytes.

Q.2. The primary purpose of software is to turn data into.

A] Website.

B] Infromation.

C] Programs.

D] Objects.

Q.3. GUI Stands for

A] Graphical User Interface.

B] Greater User Interface.

C] Graphical Union Interface.

D] Graphical User Intereat.

Q.4. Key board keys that have arrows on them are called -

A] Function Keys.

B] Navigation Keys.

C] Typewriter Keys.

D] Special purpose keys.

Q.5. ASSCII, EBCDIC and Unicode are examples of Application Software's

A] True.

B] False.

Q.6. The easiest way to access any part of the screen in the windows operating system is using the.

A] Key Board.

B] Rat.

C] Mouse.

D]] Joystick.

Q.7. A software is also called as a

A] Procedure.

B] Data.

C] Programs.

D] Information.

Q.8. Back programs make copies of the files to be used in case the original files are damaged or lost.

A] True.

B] False.

Q.9. Microprocessor is often called as CPU

A] True.

B] False.

Q.10. .... Utility identifies unnecessary files on the hard disk and erases them based on users command.

A] Backup.

B] File Compression.

C] Uninstall Programs.

D]] Disk Clean up.

Q.11. This type of software is designs to help you be more productive tasks, and is widely used in nearly every disc live and occupation.

A] Communication Software.

B] Utility Software.

C] Basic Application Software.

D] System Software.

Q.12. Minicomputers are also known as.

A] Mid Range Computers.

B] Personal Digital Computers.

C] Mainframe Computers.

D] Laptop Computers.

Q.13. Which of the following device is used to play fast games on a computers.

A] Touch Surface.

B] Touch Screen.2

C] Track Ball.

D] Joystick.

Q.14. Which of the following would not be considered as portable computer.

A] Desktop Computer.

B] Note book computer.

C] Personal Digital Assistant.

D] None of these.

Q.15. Headphone is a typical output device.

A] True.

B] False.

Q.16. Uninstall programs help us to remove unwanted programs installed in the computer.

A] True.

B] False.

Q.17. The capacity of a storage device is usually measured in terms of bytes.

A] True.

B] False.

Q.18. Capacity of the storage device is usually measured in terms of meter.

A] True.

B] False.

Q.19............. is a pointing device.

A] Mouse.

B] Printer.

C] Scanner.

D] Keyboard.

Q.20. The keyboards keys that are labelled F1, F2 and so on are called ....

A] Function Keys.

B] Numeric Keys.

C] Typewriter Keys.

D] Special purpose keys.

Q.21. The keyboard keys like Caps lock that turn on features on or off are called.

A] Function Keys.

B] Combination Keys.

C] Toggle Keys.

D] Special Purpose Keys.

Q.22. Word processing, electronic spread sheets, database managers and graphics programs are all grouped under the title.

A] Browsings Programs.

B] Operating System.

C] Application Software.

D] Data and Information.

Q.23. Keyboard, mouse, monitor, and system unit collectively also known as

A] Solid ware.

B] Software.

C] Hardware.

D] Firm ware.

Q.24. Output of an image on the monitor screen is often called soft copy.

A] True.

B] False.

Q.25. each 0 and 1 in the binary numbering system is called a bit.

A] True.

B] False.

Q.26. Catch memory is used to store most frequently accessed information from the RAM.

A] True.

B] False.

Q.27. The system board is also known as the main board or mother board.

A] True.

B] False.

Q.28. ASSCII, EBCDIC and Unicode are binary coding schemes.

A] True.

B] False.

Q.29. The keys labelled 0-9 on the keyboard are called.

A] Function Keys.

B] Numeric Keys.

C] Typewriter Keys.

D] Special purpose keys.

Q.30. A CD ROM stands for Compact Disk Read Only Memory.

A] True.

B] False.

Q.31. .... consists of step-by-step introductions that tells the computer how to complete the task.

A] Programs.

B] Hardware.

C] Data.

D] Objects.

Q.32. A CD-R stands for CD-Recordable.

A] True.

B] False.

Q.33.......... is a background soft ware that helps the computer to manage its internal resources.

A] System Software.

B] Information.

C] Objects.

D] None of these.

Q.34. Output of an image obtained using a printer is called as hard copy.

A] True.

B] False.

Q.35. Following are the file compression programs, EXCEPT

A] Win Zip.

B] RAID.

C] Win RAR.

D] PK Zip.

Q.36. A track on a disk is one of the many circular ring areas where data is written magnetically.

A] True.

B] False.

Q.37. Floppy disks are removable storage media.

A] True.

B] False.

Q.38. The keyboard keys that have arrows on them are called.

A] Function Keys.

B] Combination Keys.

C] Navigation Keys

D] Special Purpose Keys.

Q.39. Microprocessor is often called as CPU.

A] True.

B] False.

Q.40. Eight bits make up a bite.

A] True.

B] False.

Q.41. Output of an image on the monitor screen is often called hard copy.

A] True.

B] False.

Q.42.......... are graphical objects used to represent and open commonly used applications.

A] G.U.I..

B] Primers'.

C] Windows NT.

D] Icons.

Q.43. A CD-ROM means CD-RW.

A] True.

B] False.

Q.44. Data stored in RAM is

A] Is non-volatile.

B] Is only there while the power is on.

C] Remains only a few minutes after the power is turned off.

D] Is permanent and only lost in power failure.

Q.45. A CD-R stands for CD-Regional.

A] True.

B] False.

Q.46. Primary function of a monitor is to display information to the user.

A] True.

B] False.

Q.47. Random Access Memory] RAM. is .... type of memory.

A] Permanent.

B] Temporary.

C] Flash.

D] Smart.

Q.48 The external memory of the computer is present on the motherboard in the form of slots.

A] False.

B] True.

Q.49 The internal memory of the computer is present on the motherboard in the form of chips

A] True.

B] False.

Q.50 cache memory is used to store most frequently accessed information from the ram.

A] True.

B] False.

Q.1. The "System Date" and "System Time" are the date and time as maintained by the computer's internal clock.

A] True

B] False

Q.2. Disk cleanup is used to rearrange your files so that they are not broken up.

A] True

B] False

Q.3. In Window Vista a folder system is also called a "Directory System."

A] True

B] False

Q.4. "rtf" stands for "rich text format"

A] True

B] False

Q.5. You can click on.............. to learn how to use Windows Vista, obtain troubleshooting information, receive support and more.

A] "Search"

B] "Windows"

C] "Start"

D] "Help & Support"

Q.6. In MS paint to draw a curved line, we have to click the.................... Icon.

A] "Curve"

B] "Line"

C] "Polygon"

D] "Rectangle"

Q.7. .... refers to the height and width of the characters to be printed.

A] "Font Size"

B] "Border"

C] "Cell"

D] "Font Style"

Q.8. There is button which is not present on the "Title bar".

A] Minimize

B] Start

C] Maximise

D] Close

Q.9. Disk Defragmenter is used to remove unnecessary files on your hard disk to free up space and your computer run faster.

A] True

B] False

Q.10. To change the size of your picture, Select "Image Attributes" from the menu.

A] True

B] False

Q.11. To start the calculator application click "Start" and select "All Programs Accessories Calculator."

A] True

B] False

Q.12. .... can be used to create and format large and complex text documents.

A] "Calculator"

B] "WordPad"

C] "Notepad"

D] "Text Pad"

Q.13. Notepad is a basic text editor that can be used to create simple documents.

A] True

B] False

Q.14. A folder system is also called a "................"

A] "Direction System"

B] "Directory System"

C] "Directory list"

D] "Folder book"

Q.15. A folder within a folder is known as a "Folder list."

A] True

B] False

Q.17. A .... is like a container in which you can store files.

A] "Icon"

B] "document"

C] "Folder"

D] "Sheet"

Q.18. The operating system's job is .... to

A] Execute many useful commands easily.

B] to make request for service through a defined application programme interface.

C] to control the computer at the most fundamental level.

D] None of these.

Q.19. The windows interface is based on ....

A] "Graphical user Interface" or GUI

B] Application Programme Interface or] API.

C] "Clipboard"

D] None of these

Q.20. The name of a file consists of two parts, the File Name and the sub file name.

A] True

B] False

Q.21. To access the location of the particular file quickly, you create a shortcut icon for the file and place it on the desktop.

A] True

B] False

Q.22. In Windows Vista windows sidebar contains mini-programs called gadgets.

A] True

B] False

Q.23. A file created using Notepad is stored with the extension.................

.

A] ".txt"

B] ".docx"

C] ".png"

D] ".jpg"

Q.24. In windows vista two types of "searchers" are supported: Regular search Instant search.

A] True

B] False

Q.25. When your computer is booted and is ready to use, the screen you see is called the ....

A] "Table top"

B] "Desktop"

C] "Laptop"

D] None of these

Q.26. "Computer" is an application which performs functions same as that of a handheld calculator.

A] True

B] False

Q.27. .... is designed to prevent and remove spy ware.

A] User Account Control

B] Windows Firewall

C] Windows Defender

D] Parental Controls

Q.28. The clipboard is not available in Windows Vista Programs.

A] True

B] False

Q.29. What is "Windows Aero"

A] It is the graphical user interface for Windows XP.

B] It is the graphical user interface for Windows Vista.

C] Application Program

D] None of these

Q.30. Which is the basic program of a computer?

A] Operating System

B] Software Program

C] Application Program

D] None of these

Q.1. Netscape Navigator is a type of ....

A] Utility Program.

B] Operating System.

C] Browser.

D] Web Authoring Program.

Q.2. When you type an address such as "http://www.mkcl.org", in this .org indicates.

A] Original Web Site.

B] Commercial Web Site.

C] Organizational Web Site.

D] Educational Web Site.

Q.3. You can search the World Wide Web for a specific topic by using .... and.................

A] Gophers, Fido's.

B] Scanner, Search Engine.

C] Search Engines, Indexes.

D Browsers, Larkers.

Q.4. A] n. .... is a set of rules for how information and messages are sent over the internet.

A] Protocol.

B] ISP.

C] Applet.

D] HTML Hyper Text Markup Language.

Q.5. Discussion on the internet about specific topic is known as

A] News.

B] News group.

C] Veronica.

D] Telnet.

Q.6. Which of the following is not a type of protocol?

A] TCI/IP

B] ASCII

C] None of these.

D] ppp

Q.7. Which of the following is a type of protocol?

A] ASCII

B] RAM

C] TCI/IP

D] DBA

Q.8. The three parts of an e-mail message are

A] TCP/IP, Domain and ISP.

B] Destination, Device and Sender.

C] Header, Message and Signature.

D] TCP, IP and Message.

Q.9. The network connecting several computers all over the world is?

A] Intranet.

B] Internet.

C] Arpanet.

D] Network.

Q.10. Which of the following is a browser.

A] Web site.

B] Microsoft.

C] Internet Explorer.

D] www.

Q.11. The terms DNS stands for.

A] Data Naming System.

B] Do Name System.

C] Domain Name System.

D] Duplicate Name System.

Q.12. Internet e-mail address is .... for every user.

A] Unique.

B] Same.

C] Common.

D] None of these.

Q.13. For navigating any website, user has to enter

A] URL.

B] www.

C] PPP.

D] None of these.

Q.14. What is the full form of E-Commerce ?

A] English Commerce.

B] Electronic Commerce.

C] Electric Commerce.

D] Element Commerce.

Q.15. To send e-mail to someone you need ....

A] Resident Address.

B] Internet Connectivity.

C] Fax Address.

D] None of these.

Q.16. .... is used to see the web page.

A] Inbox.

B] Recycle bin.

C] Internet Explorer.
D] Network Neighbourhood.
Q.17. Full form of URL
A] Universal Resource Locator.
B] Uniform Resource Locator.
C] Uni Resource Locator.
D] None of these.
Q.18. Modem converts data from a CD to a hard disk.
A] True.
B] False.
Q.19. Which of the following is a search engine.
A] Google.
B] Alta Vista.
C] Yahoo.
D] All of these.
Q.20. What is meant by E-Commerce?
A] Online selling, purchasing, account handling etc.
B] Subject commerce stream.
C] Electronic equipment to deal with commercial problem.
D] All of the above.
Q.21. . The extensions .gov, .edu, .mil, and .net are called.
A] DNSs.
B] E-mail targets.
C] Domain codes.
D] Mail to address.
Q.22. Web spiders and crawlers are examples of
A] Browsers.
B] Search Engines.
C] HTML Programs.
D] Flames.
Q.23. What is an URL ?
A] A software package used to cruise the World Wide Web..
B] The address of a resource on the World Wide Web.
C] The terms used to describe an internal wizard.
D] A live chat program [Unlimited real time language.
Q.24. What does the abbreviation "www." stands for.
A] World Wide Web.
B] Wide Wide Web.

C] World Width Web.

D] World with Web.

Q.25. Website that allows the user to search for data on keywords is:

A] Chat engines.

B] Routers.

C] Web Server.

D] Search engines.

Q.26. Which of the following web search engine is used worldwide?

A] Domain.

B] Google.

C] Toggle.

D] None of these.

Q.27. When you use a(n) .... to search for a topic, the information you search through is organized into a database like structure.

A] Search engine.

B] Index.

C] Spider.

D] Applet.

Q.28. Which of the following system electronic letter or message sent between individuals or computers.

A] E-mail.

B] Online Service.

C] Share Resources.

D] Voice mail messaging.

Q.29. To add current web to the favourites list.

A] Click "Favourites - Add to Favourites".

B] Click "Add - Favourites.

C] Click "File - Favourites.

D] All of these.

Q.30. Moving around the web from one site to another is referred to as...............

A] Linking.

B] Navigating.

C] Hopping.

D] Paging.

Q.31. A protocol defines the rules for passing information between two or more computers.

A] True.

B] False.

Q.32. Information sent over the Internet is divided into small pieces called.

A] Packets.

B] PPPs.

C] e-mail forms.

D] Messages.

Q.33. Protocols like PPP and SLIP are used for.

A] Data Transfer.

B] Dialup internet connection.

C] Domain Registration.

D] None of these.

Q.34. The .com indicates websites of............. Types of organization.

A] Commercial.

B] Complex.

C] Company.

D] Cargo.

Q.35. Sending messages on the internet to another person's mailbox is

A] E-Business.

B] E-Letter.

C] E-Mail.

D] Cyber Mali.

www.ingramcontent.com/pod-product-compliance
Ingram Content Group UK Ltd.
Pitfield, Milton Keynes, MK11 3LW, UK
UKHW021915190726
13853UKWH00002B/680

9 798888 151907